Utopian and Critical Thinking

DUQUESNE STUDIES
Philosophical Series

29

Utopian and Critical Thinking

by

Martin G. Plattel

Duquesne University Press, Pittsburgh, Pa.
Editions E. Nauwelaerts, Louvain

DUQUESNE STUDIES
PHILOSOPHICAL SERIES

Andrew G. van Melsen and Henry J. Koren, editors.

Titles in Print

Volume Six—*P. Henry van Laer, THE PHILOSOPHY OF SCIENCE*, Part One: Science in General. Pp. XVII and 164. Second edition. Price: cloth $3.75.

Volume Eight—*Albert Dondeyne, CONTEMPORARY EUROPEAN THOUGHT AND CHRISTIAN FAITH.* Pp. XI and 211. Third impression. Price $5.75. Published also in French.

Volume Nine—*Maxwell J. Charlesworth, PHILOSOPHY AND LINGUISTIC ANALYSIS.* Pp. XIII and 234. Second impression. Price: paper $4.75, cloth $5.50.

Volume Eleven—*Remy C. Kwant, ENCOUNTER.* Pp. VIII and 85. Second impression. Price: cloth, $3.25. Published also in Dutch.

Volume Twelve—*William A. Luijpen, EXISTENTIAL PHENOMENOLOGY.* Pp. 409. Revised Edition. Price: cloth $8.95. Published also in Dutch and Spanish. German edition in preparation.

Volume Thirteen—*Andrew G. van Melsen, SCIENCE AND TECHNOLOGY.* Pp. X and 273. Price: paper $6.20, cloth $6.95. Published also in Dutch, German and Polish.

Volume Sixteen—*John A. Peters, METAPHYSICS: A SYSTEMATIC SURVEY.* Pp. XVIII and 529. Price: paper $9.00, cloth $9.75. Published also in Dutch.

Volume Seventeen—*William A. Luijpen, PHENOMENOLOGY AND ATHEISM.* Pp. XIV and 342. Second impression. Price: $4.25. Published also in Dutch.

First Printing

Library of Congress catalog card number: 72-189976

ISBN 0-8207-0143-2

PRINTED IN THE UNITED STATES OF AMERICA

CONTENTS

AUTHOR'S PREFACE

The term "utopia" has become very fashionable in the past few years. Contemporary society is in a crisis situation and demands a qualitatively different picture of the future, and this has resulted in a revival of utopian thinking. Utopian thinking is viewed as the image of the new future in which one believes. Its imaginative power develops alternatives to our situation. The social sciences are suddenly discovering that the utopian phenomenon constitutes a sociological category which they have unduly neglected. Until recently, utopian thinking was out of place in sociology. The utopian thinker was, in the eyes of the man of science, a dreamer and, consequently, uncritical. But all of a sudden the roles have been reversed. Utopian thinking turns out to be connected with critical reflection. And it is precisely the utopian thinker who now addresses to the sciences the reproach that they proceed in an uncritical fashion.

Today there is widespread opposition to a one-sided emphasis on work, there is a rebellion of the *homo ludens*, playful man. We are rediscovering that the "play" of the imagination eminently qualifies as a human activity, side by side with the "work" of the intellect. More, however, is involved than a mere revaluation of imaginative play *side by side* with intellectual work. We must get rid of the absolute opposition between play and work. Playful imagination turns out to be indispensable today for scientific work itself. Utopias result when man's imagination playfully goes to work. The utopian thinker is a man who renews society by playful thinking and

9

thoughtful playing. His utopia is a reconnaissance, an exploration orientated to a new future. The utopian horizon renews everything. The utopian expectation opens society to new possibilities of life.

This publication has been born from wonder, from the author's wondering about the fact that in the past few years the term "utopia" began to be used in all kinds of writings and discussions. His investigation of this phenomenon led him to the reflections on the category of utopian thinking contained in this study.

This work is divided into two parts. The first and larger part discusses what is meant by utopia, its properties and the demands that must be made of utopian thinking. Special attention is paid to the relationship between utopia and ideology. The second and smaller part contains a number of social-utopian essays, that is to say, critical reflections on society. Because each of these essays is self-contained, it became sometimes necessary briefly to repeat a few previously explained ideas as the background of the topic under consideration.

There exists, we think, a need for a sociological-philosophical reflection on the utopian phenomenon. Part One endeavors to help provide for this need. But any reflection on this phenomenon leads to the realization that the essence of utopia lies in praxis. That's why Part Two tries in a modest way to deal more concretely with a few particular topics.

Martin G. Plattel

TRANSLATOR'S PREFACE

This book has been translated by the undersigned and submitted to the author for his approval. Indexes have been added for the convenience of the reader. One of the essays in Part Two has been omitted because of its limited interest outside Holland. We also wish to express our thanks to Dr. James Erpenbeck for improving the readability of this translation.

Henry J. Koren

PART ONE

Utopian Thinking and Critical Thought

Introduction

There is an ever-increasing prosperity in the West but, in spite of this, there is a growing mood of discontent. A threatening by-product of prosperity turns out to be a dissatisfied society. There are many people who refuse to get excited by the prospect of a higher standard of living and a growing national product; they are no longer able to adore such gods. A large segment of the younger generation in particular no longer believes in the American way of life. They express their disenchantment by making targets of all those who occupy positions of leadership in the religious, political, military, industrial and scientific world. For the present this disenchantment expresses itself mainly in intellectual circles, particularly in our colleges and universities; thus it has not yet had any direct social consequences.

Many people, however, worry whether perhaps the colleges and universities are the locus of the abcess, the place where the waste-products of a diseased social organism force an exit. Isn't the "horn of plenty" the deceptive external facade of a society which resembles a deep-red, luscious-looking apple which is rotten at the core but manages to concentrate its last remnant of vital energy on the production of that misleading appearance? Is prosperity the masking color of a social order which in its inner bosom is afflicted with a consumptive tuberculosis?

Even if one doesn't subscribe to such a pessimistic view, it should be obvious that our society is beginning to move like a live volcano. Today's discontent doesn't appear to be a passing conjunctural phenomenon but is profoundly structural. One cannot dismiss today's rebellious trend with the remark that it merely involves a number of frustrated intellectuals and students who do not have the courage to commit themselves to our society and who rather indulge in criticizing everything from a safe distance. Externally viewed, symptoms of frustration always appear to be irrational; yet they possess a more profound meaning and must be deciphered. The extraparliamentary opposition and the increasing extraparliamentary violence must make society begin to think about the underlying causes why so many people feel alienated from society and from themselves. It is utterly inadequate merely to reject or approve the provocative actions one can witness almost every day.

1.   CRITIQUE AND CRISIS

Today's call for critical reflection and a critical view of society seems to announce an era in which there will occur a revolutionary change in outlook regarding man and society. The future, it is said, will be radically different from the present.

Critique occurs most of all when there is a critical situation, for a crisis means that the situation is critical. When society is in a state of crisis, it stands at a critical crossroads. The crisis of the ailment has then reached the point where the social organism cannot escape choosing either one way or the other. Either it opts for the road of the cure and mobilizes its reserves of vital energy for this purpose or it slowly degenerates further and dies from consumption.

The new revolutionaries are people who most strongly experience the crisis situation. Their violent feelings are the spontaneous reaction of life to the deadly danger threatening our society. These people want to open a road to a new future before it is too late to conquer the forces of death. Those youthful rebels are perhaps neither more nor less moved in the social sense than an older generation, but they wish to offer their answer to the present situation of person and society. The answer to a new situation is per force radical because a crisis situation demands a radical change of position.

There is something tragic as well as comic in the fact that people who in the past were least of all concerned about social democracy and spent their time in the pursuit of their private pleasures, now put on the mantle of the prophet when they hear revolutionary cries. They risk being false prophets because they don't understand the new spirit of the times, and by their reactionary violence they force the trailblazers of the new future to meet violence by violence.

All of us are aroused from our democratic slumber by the new and impetuous elan. Western man thought that he was democratic but, as a matter of fact, he more and more neglected his social responsibility. He withdrew within the shell of his private prosperity and private little pleasures and more or less left society to its fate. He was willing to believe in democracy if it guaranteed that his private income would annually grow by a few per cent.

All this doesn't mean that the new revolutionary interest always has its source in authentic selflessness and a well-balanced ideal. There undoubtedly are elements of regression and projection in the revolutionary protest. Thinking about the future in terms of the paradise can be a symptom of regression and a flight into the childish world of fantasy. Moreover, a defense-mechanism is often at work when one pictures the existing situation as totally evil. One then projects outside aggression in order not to notice one's own.[1]

Nevertheless, it would be wrong to appeal to such Oedipus-complexes in order to claim that one can safely disregard the cry of the critical younger generation. Precisely because they are young and still without vested interests, today's young people feel that the future of man and society is really at stake. If there are elements of regression and projection in the revolutionary protest, they are the result of the fact that a threatening and hopeless situation makes people feel ill at ease and powerless. Regression occurs precisely when one has no possibility of progressing toward adulthood, and one takes refuge in projections because one cannot identify oneself with the accepted values.

2. CRITICAL DISCONTENT

What is happening today is a cultural and political crisis. The cultural complaint refers to the problem of technocracy versus democratic freedom. There is a cultural conflict between prosperity and well-being. The second complaint is connected with the first and refers to the collective violence of the present world order. The complainants radically wish to do away with the political contrasts in our world.

Today's revolutionary thought insists in the first place on a *cultural* revolution. It is in sympathy with the cultural experiments of Castro and Mao. All contemporary complaints are concerned with the phenomenon that our unprecedented wealth of means threatens to block the road to authentically human needs. Technological and scientific progress with its rigid rationality and calculability is accompanied by an ever increasing loss of freedom. An authoritarian and technocratic system ever more deprives man of his autonomy. And this happens precisely when the means to create a new world are available.

To point out that this danger exists is nothing new. In his *Utopia* Thomas More already argued that at a given moment production must be restricted for the sake of other human values. Man's attitude toward the goods of this world will always remain essentially ambiguous. Alienation is necessarily the ever-present background of all material domination and control. Thus it must be granted that any technological domination always has certain problematic aspects. Today, however, the delicate balance involved in any such domination is in danger of being fundamentally disrupted. For society does not determine the goals of its technological power; on the contrary, the established technological structure imposes the laws of its own blind inner development on society and alienates man.

In the past also society always existed in an antagonistic pose: one social class opposed itself to the others as an authoritarian father and exploited them. Every revolution of the oppressed class in the past has also always remained a betrayed revolution because it took over the father role of the other class. The feudal lords oppressed the burghers, but when the burghers rose in revolt and conquered, they became bourgeois and oppressed the proletarians. People have always been afraid of the fatherless society and democratic brotherhood.

Today, however, there are many who think that our contemporary society is totally alienating. It is no longer a matter of one group oppressing the other, but the very technico-economic system itself turns against man and alienates him from himself.

When toward the end of the nineteenth century science and technical skill united, technological rationality began indeed to reach ever farther. A threefold technical development was involved in this. Technology aims, first of all, at the development of the forces of production, secondly, at the organization of the relationships of production, and finally at the regulation of social relationships.[1]

The three phases can be roughly divided as follows. The first spectacular growth in the realm of technological control began around 1880 and lasted till about World War I. It was the period of the production of machines, which gave rise to economic concentrations and enormous business enterprises. The period between the two world wars shows the birth of the technique of organization. Because the technical forces of production were very expensive, the relationships of production had to be guided according to rational methods of labor.

After World War II a third technical acceleration has occurred, so-called "human engineering," which regulates social relationships. The inexorable technical growth of the forces of production and capital goods and the further rationalization of the relationships of production and enterprises now demand that the social behavior of man be regulated. The giant industrial companies make investments which force them to take a long-range view of things. Formerly planning aimed only at internal affairs, and social relationships were viewed as given data. Now, however, external affairs also have to be dealt with, and the management of these external affairs is becoming just as important as that of internal business. To safeguard the continuity of the enterprises, the sale of products must be made secure, and this means that the consumer must be manipulated. The offer of means of production, particularly that of labor, needs to be planned. An appeal has to be made to the government for the education of this labor pool. By its conjunctural and structural policies the State must guarantee the markets of both purchases and sales.

The techno-structure manipulates the behavior of the citizen, the consumer, the industrialist and the worker. The world which we ourselves have produced imposes itself on us, so that we become a product of our own products. The universal extension of technology is at cross purposes with its own original goal. Introduced to liberate man from the enslaving forces of want and scarcity, technology increasingly moves into the opposite direction and enslaves man to itself. But, thanks to a defense-mechanism built into the system, man is not conscious of this alienation. Even as formerly religion sometimes served as the opium of the people which masked their oppression, so now consumption has become in our economic system the opiate that is used to prevent the people's repression from revealing itself.

Oft-quoted and sometimes honored as a prophet, Herbert Marcuse in particular is very pessimistic in this matter.[2] In his view repression is much more profound than ever before. At the time of Marx, he says, there was only partial oppression—the capitalistic group exploited the proletarian group. But by its totalitarian character the modern prosperity State holds everyone in its clutches. The proletarians have made a fetish of consumption, they are thereby alienated and have lost their revolutionary birthright. One could object that Marcuse indulges in simplifying exaggerations; nevertheless, it remains true that the huge sales of his work prove at least that today there is widespread discontent with the existing state of affairs.

The prosperity State is already partly caught in the fatal spiral in which the ever-increasing rate of production drives consumption to higher levels while, on the other hand, the newly acquired patterns of consumption in their turn accelerate production. There is too much blind obedience to the laws of economic growth.

Man originally developed an apparatus of production to take care of existing needs, but now the production apparatus artificially nurses new needs in order to maintain production. In this way the needs of the entire society are subjected to goals imposed by the blind and autonomous development and expansion of industrial enterprises.[3]

The accelerated race between producers and consumers leads to the exhaustion of society. Our philosophy of production easily creates dissatisfied people. One may ask whether our Western economy hasn't reached the stage where brakes have to be applied to the prosperity race. According to J. Henry, American society doesn't draw its inspiration from genuinely human values but from an artificial stimulation of material needs. He speaks of a "driven culture" and a "deliberate creation of needs."[4] It is a fact that in the U.S.A. the most ridiculous consumer items are produced at a time when man's primary needs in housing, clothing and food are not yet adequately taken care of for at least fifteen per cent of the population.

The old story of King Midas has been forgotten. When he was permitted to ask the gods a favor, Midas requested that whatever he touched would be changed into gold. Midas is the paradigm of the *homo economicus*. He soon begged the gods to be relieved of that favor, for his food as well as his beloved wife changed into blocks of gold. King Midas could no longer satisfy his genuinely human needs of food and love, so that he was in peril of perishing both physically and mentally.

The economic passion to appropriate and possess ever more things leads to a system in which people dominate other people. Man is in danger of forgetting that his happiness and his freedom have their creative source in the peaceful togetherness with others. In relating to the other face to face, I discover the origin and meaning of my life. When I look at the naked and defenseless face of the other, I experience that life ultimately doesn't mean economic power, economic struggle and the war of competition but is ordered to peace and humanity.[5]

Today's uneasiness in the Western world and in Eastern Europe finds expression in the complaint that culture is too much determined by "economism." Capitalism and Marxism are two variations of the same system, and in both human freedom is too much strangled by considerations of usefulness and economic achievement. In the West people are manipulated by the world of business, but in Eastern Europe the same kind of manipulation is performed by the authoritarian and bureaucratic State.

Today's revolutionary impetus insists also on a *political* revolution. There is a growing consciousness of social responsibility. The evolution that has occurred in this respect is remarkable. In the prewar years the older generation also adopted a social attitude and aimed at providing work and income for the people of one's own country. Attempts were made to foster social justice but in a national perspective. But following World War II, the prewar generation more and more withdrew into the sphere of private concerns. This withdrawal had both positive and negative aspects. For the first time, a generation that had experienced the plague of unemployment and poverty was able to enjoy prosperity. On the other hand, the private-social sphere served as a compensation for the growing anonymity and bureaucratization of the new social order.

Today's generation, however, again places greater emphasis on social responsibility. Just as the democratic ethic of an older generation refused to treat workers as second class citizens, so now the same democratic sentiment demands that poor nations be not treated as second class countries. Social justice has extended its range of action from citizenship of a State to world citizenship.

Contemporary neo-Marxist thought rightly objects to certain one-sided aspects of the existentialistic philosophy which became fashionable in Western Europe after World War II. Existentialistic personalism overemphasized the authenticity of the person in the private sphere; it overstressed the I-you relationship at the expense of the political and social dimension. While this personalism deserves praise for developing a "micro-ethics" of interhuman relationships, it neglected the "macro-ethics" pertaining to the events happening in the social world at large.[6]

Overemphasis on human subjectivity has also often led to pseudo-concreteness in existential phenomenology. The existentialistic view of man paid too much attention to authentic existence, to acting as one who has come of age in no matter what situation. If only one took up his existence in freedom, it did not matter what he did with this freedom. Thus human subjectivity easily evaporated into a purely formal and empty *a priori* attitude. The story told about one of Heidegger's students is typical in this respect. This young man claimed that he was "firmly resolved," although he did not yet know what he had resolved.

In today's philosophy the social and political dimensions are rightly placed in the center of attention. Neo-Marxism stresses the content of authentic existence, the importance of social situations and structures for man's endeavor to become himself. Many progressive people today look upon the existential philosophy which flourished after World War II in Europe as a philosophical alienation. They view it as an attempt to confer a semblance of freedom and authenticity upon man in the private sphere, so as to counteract the influence of today's anonymous and bureaucratic society.

The reproach of Neo-Marxism that existentialism has remained too much a bourgeois philosophy is not entirely unjustified. Bourgeois thinkers of the Enlightenment maintained a rigorous separation between morality and politics.[7] Morality was relegated from the domain of politics and shut up in the private realm of man's inner conscience. The new philosophical trends, however, should be on guard lest they fall into the opposite extreme. It is true that the person cannot achieve freedom if the existing structures are not modified, but new structures do not lead to a new man without any further ado. Both persons and structures must be modified. The structural and the personalistic approach must closely interlock. At present, attention is mainly directed to the structures because they possess such a supra-individual power that they prevent man from becoming conscious of himself on a personal level.

That's why the revolutionary impetus aims at democratizing the existing institutions. It argues that such a democratization is very important for man's freedom. The State, the people or the nation have value only to the extent that they are frameworks which help enlarge and deepen liberty, equality and fraternity in the world. Although the French Revolution proclaimed the democratic equality of men, the honor of the nation, country or State continued to rank above the dignity of the person. Two disastrous world wars have made us experience how over and over again the concrete and individual person is sacrificed to the absolute totality of the State or nation.[8]

The desire for a democratic socialism is not an invention of abstract philosophical thought, but truly expresses the way our time views life. This point may be illustrated by the following story. A few years ago a violent debate raged at one of Germany's universities. The names of those who had fallen in World War II had been carved in the stonewall of one of the buildings, together with the famous verse of Horace: *Dulce et decorum est pro patria mori* (It is sweet and honorable to die for the fatherland). When a few students covered Horace's words with a piece of cloth, a discussion arose about that sentence and soon became very acrimonious. Should that text be removed or not? In an open debate attended by many students passions ran very high. Those opposed to the removal argued that respect for the dead who had so heroically laid down their lives demanded that Horace's words be left standing. The others declared themselves against any form of hero-worship which could be exploited in favor of a political party such as that of the Nazis. The conflict seemed insoluble. Then the university rector proposed that the offending works be replaced by the text: *Mortui viventes obligant* (The dead impose a duty on the living). His proposal met at once with universal applause. This was a duty which all were willing to recognize. The students had merely vented their critical mood. They were against romanticism, particularly the dangerous type in which death in defense of political structures is exalted as heroism.

Today's world order is still based on the antiquated political structures of "inside" versus "outside," of our State or power block versus that of the others. Justice and solidarity for those "inside" continue to be accompanied by conquest and violence with respect to those "outside." The world is divided into power blocks which strengthen the "inside" prosperity, solidarity and security by "outside" economic exploitation and hostility. One group's national or continental interests are pursued at the expense of the national or continental interests of the others, such as the third world.[9]

Precisely now that the world turns out to be technically and economically a single whole in which all parts depend on all other parts, the antiquated political institutions of "inside" versus "outside" lead to violence on a major scale. Structural violence and structural injustice increase as the institutions of the political suprastructure continue to maintain their autonomy at the expense of one another in a world in which there really is no longer room for "inside" versus "outside" dimensions on the infrastructural level. Today's political structures with their world-wide channels of communication are in possession of the means to enlarge their "outside" conquests. The antiquated structures of "inside" versus "outside" preserve and increase the unjust distribution of prosperity in the world and the insane arms race. It is institutional inertia rather than the violence of man which ails the world today.

The enlarged scale of violence against the "outside" tends to reduce the "inside" itself to a mere shell. In his famous work *The New Industrial State*, John K. Galbraith warns of the danger that we will end up with a system that is democratic in name only. The giant capitalistic enterprises of the West and the State monopolies of the East threaten to determine the socio-political goals of human society. The revolutionary political changes of our time demand a radical democratization with respect to both "inside" and "outside."

3. THE REBIRTH OF THE SOCIAL UTOPIA

No matter what one thinks about the provocative protests and the extraparliamentary opposition, one thing is certain—we live today in a situation of social crisis. The unquestioned answers that used to be commonly accepted in the past no longer suffice. The social values on which the edifice of our society is built are subject to doubt in our day. We stand at a turning point in history, a point at which a new appreciation of man and a new vision of society are trying to break through.

In this context it is illustrating that in the past few years there has been a revaluation of social-utopian thinking. The utopian mood and utopian style of writing always flourish at revolutionary turning points of human history. In 1955 Fred Polak published his masterful study *The Image of The Future*, and wrote about the broken future of Western culture. He complained there that our civilization no longer has any vision of the future and noted that our society stands for a critical choice: either on to new heights or to ever greater decay. He concluded with the warning: "If the prevailing fashion of inverting utopian thinking, of successively taking a negative attitude toward all pictures of the future, continues, then the prospect facing us is that of the further degeneration and ultimate doom of Western civilization."[1] But in his later work *Prognostics*, published in 1968, the same author speaks about the rebirth of the future. He points out that the change occurred around 1960, when the utopian-idealistic vision of the future was rehabilitated.[2]

Utopian writings always are far ahead of their time. For example, Thomas More in his *Utopia* (1526) saw the end of feudalism and nobility and anticipated the coming of capitalistic production. Similarly, the era of the Enlightenment in the eighteenth century meant the definitive end of the medieval religious worldview with its belief in authority. The utopian literature of that era produced wondrous stories of travel, planetary novels and predictions of the future, thus projecting the image of our technological civilization. Utopian writings make it possible for society to face the future in a creative fashion and to bring new ideas to realization.

Thus it is not surprising that the critical way of thinking which is now arising assumes a protesting and utopian attitude toward the existing situation. Man and society, so it says, must undergo a psychoanalytic and socioanalytic cure in order to become conscious of the repressive and manipulative features of present-day structures. What is involved in this protest is a revolt of the creative man; he wishes to remain a "being of possibilities" and to retain a choice of alternatives. Utopian thinking, as a play of fancy and imagination, wants to break through and transcend the existing order which is one-sidedly based on the "performance principle." It tries to create elbow room for the repressed "pleasure principle" in the existing institutions. The utopian way of thinking, which starts from the assumption that "things could be different,"[3] wishes to save man from "establishments."

The utopian sketch of a possible future raises questions about the existing form of society. In the light of a concrete utopia society can become conscious of the oppression, exploitation and inertia existing in its midst.

Utopian ways of thinking or writing occupy a central position in contemporary critical thought. In the Hegelian-Marxist trend of thinking followed by Bloch, Marcuse and Kofler a normative function is ascribed to utopian thought. Bloch's standard work, *The Principle of Hope*, presents a complete philosophy of the utopian dimension.[4] The utopian *novum* constitutes the dynamic force of every new development. According to Bloch, it is the medium through which things that haven't yet reached consciousness obtain a chance to unfold themselves dynamically. And in his book *Eros and Civilization* Marcuse ascribes a liberating power to utopian thinking with respect to the fixating principle of reality. Freedom, he holds, is conceivable only as the realization of that which today is still called utopian. Utopian thought, as a playing with possibilities, exercises a critical function by putting itself negatively and dialectically in opposition to the existing situation. Marcuse refers to the logic of protest, dialectical negation and critical negativity when he wishes to indicate the revolutionary impetus of utopian thinking. And in his work *The Ascetical Eros* Kofler dwells extensively on the difference between the erotic delight and the ascetical discipline in the utopian and the antagonistic societies.[5]

The value of the utopian approach, as the play of fancy, intuition and imagination, is stressed also by writers who do not indulge in Hegelian-Marxist dialectics. For example, R. Ruyer refers to the function of what he calls the "utopian way."[6] And F. Polak views the utopian procedure as a meaningful tool to investigate the future. Tillich dwells on the political importance of utopian thought, for "man does not have the potential for this or that particular thing but . . . he has 'the potential,' he is the being which is capable of transcending what is given and to keep doing this without limit."[7]

Plessner thinks that in utopian thought man with his "eccentric positionality" tests and pursues "the possibility that things could be different."[8] The social sciences in particular place increasingly more emphasis on the function of social imagination. Now that society is orientated to the future and constitutes a dynamic process through which a world of meaning is established, sociology, if it does not wish merely to dwell on the *status quo*, needs "creative utopian thinking" (D. Riesman),[9] "sociological imagination" (C. Wright Mills),[10] and "social fancy" (R. Jungk).[11]

The mere fact that our time loves to speak about this future in utopian terms indicates that a radical change is involved. The new society cannot be brought about by a number of partial reforms within the existing framework. The utopian approach expresses its aspirations by projecting a new totality. It is not interested in restoring an old building but in a revolutionary new edifice, a "utopian concrete totality."[12] As Kolakowski succinctly puts it, "The 'Left' secretes utopias as the pancreas secretes insulin."[13] The word "Left" here doesn't refer to the left wing sector of the existing political order but to the "New Left" in both the Western system of private capitalism and the East-European system of State capitalism. In the eyes of the utopian left, the Soviet Union with its dogmatic Marxism is just as much to the right and just as atrophied as are other rightist parties.

The increasing secularization of our contemporary view of man and the world serves to stimulate the importance attached to the function of utopian thinking. Even in the classical utopias this tendency existed already in a hidden way. The utopian imagination is born from man's desire to bring about his own happiness by his own creative endeavors. Utopian thought is essentially humanistic insofar as it implies an act of faith in man and doesn't start from the premise that man's life is immutably fixed. Utopian thinking is also demiurgic in the sense that man himself wishes to bring about a better world.

In this utopian venture, this movement of emancipation, one can also hear constant warnings against presumption on the part of man. The utopian thinker must practice restraint and remain a realistic utopian. The utopian explorer must sail exactly in between the rock of petrifaction and the whirlpool of chaos. The old utopias showed how man could come into conflict with the gods and be severely punished for his brashness. Utopian pride comes before the fall. One can think here of Adam and Eve, of Prometheus and Icarus. But modern utopian novels, such as Huxley's *Brave New World* and Orwell's *1984*, also warn man to practice a measure of self-restraint in his technical power. They also contain an admonition to observe the boundaries between what is possible and what is permissible, and a plea not to become a Lucifer or a Prometheus. The modern utopian explorer, too, must maneuver in between the rock of Scylla and the whirlpool of Charibdis.

4. THE HISTORY OF UTOPIAN THINKING

Utopia with its expectation of a better man and a better world always intends to transcend given reality; it refuses to be satisfied with the existing situation. The utopia strives for the ideal of harmony and reconciliation. Utopian imagination dreams of another and better future than the present. It looks at man in the future and discloses the coming ideal society to today's man. Utopian imagination goes beyond the limited world in the direction of the unlimited; it transcends the imperfect condition of the present and moves toward greater perfection and greater harmony.

The utopian story, as a process of transcendence, thus is a historical phenomenon, one whose form and content vary according to the situation from which it arises and which it transcends. It assumes different forms in an era when man thinks that he himself must take charge of his future than in a period in which the traditions of the past strongly continue to control man's view of life. A brief historical sketch can help us to discern with greater clarity the main tenor of the utopian man throughout the varying historical forms of utopian writings. What interests us here are the lines of development and not an encyclopedic exposition about the content of the many utopian books.[1]

In classical Antiquity the utopian work, in the specific sense of a literary or scientific genre, did not yet explicitly occur. Nevertheless,

it is largely in Antiquity that we must look for the origin of the utopian intention as man's attempt to shape his own future. Ancient
Hellas lived by its vision of the future. Greek culture offers a fas-
cinating picture of how man endeavored to escape from superhuman
and mythical powers in order to take charge of his own future. The
heroes in Homer's epics and in the Greek tragedies manfully struggle against a ruthless fate. They are lost before they begin, but in
their defeat they remain victors. In their struggle against superhuman powers the Greek heroes show a human power.[2]

The philosophy of ancient Greece slowly managed to break away
from the world of myth and magic. Human thought pushed back
the world dominated by a pitiless fate. A philosophical world-view
gradually replaced the mythological view. The mythical fate was
replaced by the idea of a harmonious world order, which from above
and from without permeates everything. This cosmic harmony vertically determines the here and now of man. The utopian pictures
of the future dating from that time already endeavor to bring this
transcendent order within man's reach; they horizontally project
the vertical harmony of the cosmos.

For example, in his *Republic* Plato presents the utopian model of
the State, he sketches an ideal society within the framework of the
polis, the city-State. In the myth the supra-historical fate fully determines the "somewhere" of man, but in the *Republic* the utopian
"nowhere" of the ideal society transcends the existing "somewhere"
of the city-State. Although the utopian land of "nowhere" is an un-
attainable ideal, it is nevertheless dreamt about on the basis of man's
"somewhere."

Myth and utopia still remain closely connected here. The vertical
determination by the myth still makes itself strongly felt, as is evident from this that the world of the Idea, in the sense of all-encompassing eternal and divine justice, functions as the model of human
society. Plato's State tries to realize this divine Idea of justice in this
world. The static-cosmic world order is the divine exemplar of a
utopically projected static and autarkical State. In Greek culture the
ideal harmony stands high above this world but, on the other hand,
it eminently applies to this world.

The Christian Middle Ages did not directly know utopian pictures of the future. For medieval man his destiny lay in the hands of God rather than his own. But even there the utopian mood made itself occasionally felt. For instance, the monk Joachim of Fiore (ab. 1130-1202) modified the Christian eschatology with its expectation of the final time after the end of world history into an expectation of salvation within the world. Joachim divided history into three periods or reigns. The first is that of the Father and covers the period of the Old Testament; it is the reign of the flesh and the law. The second is that of the Son, the period of the New Testament from Jesus Christ. It is a mixture of flesh and the spirit and it is governed by the Church and its priests. The third period is that of the Spirit, which will begin around 1260 and be entirely spiritual. The sacerdotal Church will then vanish, and mankind will constitute a single universal Christian brotherhood.

The chiliastic trends in the Middle Ages, which appealed to the vision of John's book of Revelation, also clearly show utopian aspects. Chiliasm expected an early reign of Christ before the Last Judgment. A kingdom lasting a thousand years was to come and it would be characterized by peace and justice. The numerous mendicant orders of the Middle Ages with their spirit of brotherhood and their community of goods also constituted a critical-utopian counterpart to the conditions then prevailing.

When in the Middle Ages people thought about the future, the result was a blend of transcendent eschatology and humanitarian utopian ideas. That's why social protest against the existing injustice and the desire for a better world—two elements which are eminently utopian—constantly gave rise to a revival of chiliasm. Medieval man, however, viewed his life as determined by God and therefore did not himself strive for the future; he hoped that the eschatological promise would partly be fufilled by Christ here on earth.[3]

The "New Era" begins around the sixteenth century with Columbus, Copernicus, Galileo and others. In this period man comes out of the trusted shell of the cosmos and himself tries to plan the world. This era of the Renaissance can best be characterized as the classical period of utopian thought. It was Thomas More who with his *Utopia* (1516) introduced the literary style of utopian writing.

The medieval pattern of life, based on the idea of a transcendent and divine Providence, begins to deteriorate. The Renaissance breaks away from the axiom that the lot of man and society is immutably set by God and must simply be accepted. The will to change one's social position is no longer viewed as a revolt against God. Man begins to believe in himself and views the building of the world as something for which he himself is responsible. The Renaissance gave the first impetus to a different view of man and world. It sought its inspiration for the future in the humanism of classical Antiquity. The Renaissance is the period in which man begins to struggle for his own future. This basic theme is already manifest in the *Utopia* of More, the precursor of the New Era. The Platonic model of the State was still in a certain sense an idea thought to be *above* reality, but More's *Utopia* is taken out of the realm of ideas and fictitiously placed *side by sid*e with the reality of human conditions.[4]

The Copernican revolution in the way man experienced his life also produced a drastic change in utopian reflection upon the future. The utopian writers of that time expressed a different attitude of service toward God, showed a different way of conceiving man's power with respect to the universe, and dreamt of a different kind of society.

Columbus's discovery of the New World and Copernicus's theory of the planets presented new utopian vistas. The influence of physical science and technique, which in principle opened the road to new discoveries, made itself strongly felt in utopian literature. Until the seventeenth century there was very little utopian writing about technical possibilities—at least if we except the Franciscan friar Roger Bacon (1214-1294), who boldly dreamt of ships sailing the seas without oarsmen, horseless carriages racing over the roads, and flying machines cleaving the air like birds. But after 1600 the picture changes considerably. Utopian writers like Thomas Campanella (1568-1639), Francis Bacon (1561-1626) and Cyrano de Bergerac

(1620-1655) showed great interest in the technical possibilities which were slowly beginning to emerge. The Dominican Campanella in his *City of the Sun* was keenly interested in the physical sciences which had begun to flourish with the Renaissance. Among other things he mentions shock-therapy and psychedelic or mind-enlarging means. In his *Novum Organon* and even more in his unfinished *Nova Atlantis* Francis Bacon presents the picture of an ideal society which is not governed by politicians but by a select company of men devoted to the new sciences. The discoveries of Galileo and Copernicus inspire Cyrano to write his utopian stories about travel to lunar states and solar kingdoms. These novels, which are a blend of irony and science, intend to make the reader realize that the world contains more possibilities and more space than man has hitherto believed.

Yet the new way of looking at man and the world did not easily achieve a breakthrough. The utopian writings of these centuries showed only the first signs of the new spirit of the times, which began to flourish under the influence of the sciences and the great explorations. They concentrated their attention on man's own creative power. But all this was only a hesitant beginning. The Renaissance was only an intermediary era; its spirit oscillates between that of the Middle Ages and that of the Enlightenment. Man still stood with one foot in the past while hesitantly trying to find a foothold on the path of progress. Eschatology and utopia still go hand in hand. For example, Thomas More's *Utopia* is still a secularized form of God's kingdom at the end of times. The Christian idea of eternity is here utopically projected on the world. Such fictitious or visionary stories about definitive conditions of happiness represent the classical utopian style of thinking. The eschatological utopias of the Renaissance express man's desire to take control of his own destiny but they remain dependent on the religious sphere of life which they wish to transcend. Utopian imagination anticipates the eschatological idea of God's kingdom at the end of the times and idyllically dreams about a state of happiness in this world. The Renaissance utopias are animated by a nostalgic desire for a perfect and definitive condition in the guise of a paradise. They

wish to do away with the limitations of the traditional cosmic order
but can accomplish it only as a wishful dream. The unrealistic aspect
of creative imagination still holds sway here. While the ironic
element of critique on their own time is undoubtedly present, utopian writings still remain mostly a matter of wishful dreaming and
a pleasant pastime.

The Enlightenment in the eighteenth century meant a new bloom
of utopian writing. Some people even call this period rather than
the Renaissance the classical period of utopian thought. All manner
of varieties are represented: wondrous travel tales, Robinson Cru-
soe stories, Arcadias, planetary novels, pictures of the future, ideal
societies, etc.[5] This variegated wealth is a result of the tendency to
emancipation which characterized the Enlightenment. Man breaks
definitively with belief on authority and himself sets out to explore
and investigate. The transcendent governance of the world is wholly
changed into an immanent development. Although a God continues
to be accepted as the Supreme Being, the autonomous development
of earthly reality is sufficiently safeguarded; mankind is able to help
itself through the light of reason. For example, Adam Smith, whose
Wealth of Nations made him the founder of the science of economics, believed in the rationality of a natural economic order, even
though this order is guided by God's "hidden hand." For the Enlightenment starts from the assumption that there exists a "natural
order," the working of which can be understood by man's reason.
The rigorous laws governing the events of nature apply also to society. That's why Adam Smith thinks that the economy will manifest an harmonious obedience to laws if only man's natural and rational self-interest can prevail through total and free competition.
A kind of ontological optimism is involved in this.

In this way the enlightened faith in reason and nature stimulated
utopian writing. The era was characterized by the utopia of reason.
The imagination no longer nourished itself fictitiously with paradiselike distant vistas but anticipated the progress to be made in
time. One can apply here Victor Hugo's dictum: "Today's utopia is
tomorrow's truth." The utopian genre presents a picture of the pro-

gressive development of reality in accordance with established laws. Utopia (*no* place) is here most of all *eutopia* (a *good* place). Its orientation has changed from theological to teleological.[6]

In this century, however, the function of science continued to be limited to the discovery and explanation of the world. Scientific theory and technical experiment had not yet joined hands in this era, so that the world could merely be explained but not yet changed. The enlightened explaining and exploring merely dislodged the boundaries of what is known, but not yet those of what is. The possibilities to be discovered still lay somewhere in an unexplored region of nature. In all this there is a clear-cut difference from the later experimental science of the late nineteenth century which itself projects possibilities and makes nature subservient to man.

The utopian thinking of the time also is clearly characterized by this idea of *discovery* and *explanation*.[7] The utopian possibilities are discovered, not made. The "extraordinary travels" and planetary novels of Gabriel de Foigny, Voltaire, Robert, Swift and others express the desire to go and explore unknown but pre-existing regions. The utopian visions of the future are based on the belief that the progress of knowledge will of itself lead mankind to total civilization. If the forces of nature are not disturbed, history will move ever upward in a homogeneous way and thus approach the final stage ever more closely. All this is especially clear in Morelly, who summarized the fundamental principles of his ideal society under the title *Code of Nature*. Socialists like Saint-Simon and Fourier also had a utopian trust in man's natural goodness. They conceived the perfect society as a symmetrically planned garden with reason as its architect.

Thus the belief in progress of this socialism also speaks about places of happiness and prosperity. This belief is a curious product of the rationalism and romanticism which are constantly exhibited in the Enlightenment. But there is an important difference from the paradiselike islands of the Renaissance. The earlier writers had told about fictitious places of happiness more or less in the spirit of pastime. They experienced their idyllic dreams of the future as playful substitutes for the existing imperfections and injustices of the present. The rationalistic faith in progress had less feeling for this playfulness and believed in an impending state of happiness. The utopian world was no longer far beyond reach. Its realization could be looked forward to because of the existing confidence that the world was continuously making progress toward its final completion.

This utopian rationalism remained influential deep into the nineteenth century. It exists in an unacknowledged form in Hegel, Spencer and Marx. Hegel, and to a lesser extent also Marx, was unable to escape from thinking in the absolute terms of a utopian apotheosis. Although Marxism attacked the utopian socialists because of their lack of scientific objectivity, its own scientific socialism remained a wishful dream clad in a scientific garment. Marx's socialism believes in the utopia of reason and of development according to natural laws; thus he was an adherent of utopian rationalism. While Marx declined to give a detailed picture of the final stage of communism, he was nonetheless convinced that this phase must come about with inevitable necessity, even though it is true that the oppressed class must foster the revolution and take advantage of the development of affairs. The Marxist picture of the future has the ambivalent character of an eschatology poured into a utopian mold.

The end of the nineteenth century broke with the spirit of the Enlightenment. The rationalistic optimism and expectation of progress, still manifest in Bellamy's work *Looking Backward 2000-1887* (1888), disappears around the turn of the century. Hereafter the future lies open to man's power. Progress no longer occurs as a matter of course and according to ironclad laws of nature. Science and technique begin to be attuned to each other and, as a result, society slowly acquires the power to assume control over its own future. Economic and technological power replace economical and technical "laws of nature." Secularization continues and the belief that history has a meaning independent of man loses ground. Nietzsche's *Will to Power* expresses this shift from the objective laws to the subjective aspect of man's actions. The future lies open to man as a bundle of many possibilities. There is an increasing sense of relativity but at the same time also fear that the possible developments may assume a chaotic character.

A parallel shift occurs in the realm of utopian writings. Unlike the period of the Enlightenment, utopian interest no longer seeks to *find* new possibilities but tends to *make* and *create* them. Socio-political and technico-scientific utopias influence one another. They present an anticipating picture of a future which man himself must plan.

The idea that the future lies entirely open to man began to be voiced as early as the beginning of the nineteenth century.[8] A first example of the new utopian style is offered by Erskine. In his two-volume work *Armata* (1817), he speaks about the discovery of a new power which will drive the machines and make manual labor superfluous. Science no longer has only the task of explaining the world and technique is no longer limited to an artificial imitation of nature's laws. Erskine thinks that the world will acquire a new visage through the power of scientific and technical achievements. Similarly, Cabet, in his *Voyage to Icaria, a Philosophical and Social Novel*, views technological production as the revolutionary power which makes it possible for his Icarian society to be prosperous and happy. And Jules Vernes' wondrous travels, again, do not tell us about the discovery of new countries and unknown human races but prophetically describes new inventions.

The utopian writers are no longer exclusively interested in the problems of organizing socio-political life, they are also concerned with the spiritual and biological consequences of technical inventions for human life as such. Science fiction, which anticipates future developments of science, technology and society begins to flourish in this period. H. G. Wells (1866-1946) is considered to be the founder of this type of utopian writing. In America also science fiction began to develop at the end of the nineteenth century. The principal topics are the exploration and conquest of space, the visit or invasion by intelligent beings from other planets, the robot, the city of the future, changes in the human race, and a new world war.

The characteristic feature of this period is that, unlike earlier utopias, it does not bring the movement of history to a standstill by absolutizing certain things. The future remains open to revolutionary developments. The visions of the future, no matter how fantastic they may be, are partly based on anticipations supported by the present.

The realization that man himself must shape the formless future can also be frightening. Man can experience a certain helplessness with respect to the new and unknown. When around 1900 society acquires a dimension of openness through the evolution of science and technology, the anti-utopian type of utopian writing is born. This anti-utopia looks back to the past. Against mechanization and rationalization, it appeals to the "good old times" when love, poetry, romanticism and Christian faith prevailed. Benson's *The Lord of the World*, Forster's *The Machine Stops* and Kellermann's *The Tunnel* deal in succession with the threat of technology for the Church, nature and civilization. But after 1914 the opposition between utopian and anti-utopian writings disappears. It is no longer technology and science as such that are viewed with disfavor, but only the danger which could result from the wrong use of these powers. Huxley's *Brave New World*, Orwell's *1984* and Stapleton's *Last and First Man* neither long for the past nor make a fortress of the present. These writers start from the assumption that the future lies open to man's intervention. But they are not unqualifiedly optimistic about man's culture and fear the many dangers of the new developments.[9]

After 1945 a new phase begins, one which can be characterized as a decline of utopian thinking. Obviously the date 1945 should not be taken literally. The domination of technocratic thinking in this period, strictly speaking, had its starting point already in the marriage of science and technique which occurred around the turn of the century. Today's technocracy, as has already been pointed out, is the merger of three technical developments, viz., of technology in the narrow sense, which went from machines to atomic energy and automation, secondly, the technique of organization with its planning and routing in the direction of operational research and linear programming, and thirdly, the technique of influencing social behavior.

The universal extension of the functional view leads, according to Robert Jungk, to a technocratic totalitarianism. Society is conceived in terms of system and organization models. A clear example is offered by Talcott Parsons' structural functionalism. As a matter of fact, the accelerated technological development after 1945 gives society the features of a futureless system which tries to reproduce itself with the least possible friction. To be rational thus means to see to it that all parts function as smoothly as possible within the totality. The unexpected and the new must be brought under control as much as possible according to plan. Game theories and decision-making games are developed in order to calculate within the system the uncertainties and contingencies of human behavior. The ideal of plan-controlled rationality leads in fact to a glorification of the *status quo*. The theories of growth have no other goal than to calculate fixed quotas of growth for the various parts of the accepted system. Changes are merely thought of in terms of quantitative growth. The theory of the dynamic equilibrium is actually the dynamics of a static system.[10]

Such a system analysis is little interested in the phenomenon of utopian thinking; it is even hostile to it. It views utopian preoccupations as a romantic and unscientific pursuit. For functional thinking any explanation must assume the character of a model; otherwise it is meaningless. Because reason thus stays aloof from utopian imagination, the latter usually lives a life of its own. The socio-political function of the utopian approach falls into the background. The imagination expresses itself merely in science fiction and gets lost in supra-earthly dreams of fancy.

While in the preceding centuries eschatology developed into earthly utopias, utopian thinking now assumes supra-earthly eschatological features. It views eschatological conditions in biological and technological perspectives, with the result that the tension between reality and utopia begins again to increase. Utopian writers such as Tarde and Hudson around the turn of the century had already abandoned the realistic starting point of the utopia and let their fancy play with different types and kinds of human beings on the basis of biological and technological data. Especially American science fiction after World War II went so far beyond the limits of earthly existence that it vanished into the mist of timeless and spaceless worlds.

Science fiction in this way became sheer entertainment literature, interested only in technical adventures and loves stories without any socio-political overtures. The novel here is the main thing, and the utopian character is purely incidental. The literary form of utopian writing becomes the content and the stylistic medium is raised to the level of the goal.[11] The utopian content of such writings sinks even below the level of the classical literary genre of More and Campanella, for the literary genre of the Renaissance had at least a critical social inspiration.

In the 1960s, however, there arose again a renewed interest in social utopias. The desire for a qualitatively different future inspired many people to assume a critical attitude with respect to society. Utopian writings usually are born from a need, a want. Our time produces utopias not so much because it desires but because it must. The profound social conflict and the far-reaching elimination of potential ways of life everywhere gives rise to a growing uneasiness. Tempestuous developments occur in the realm of the sciences, but there is no clear orientation to the future. Science keeps shifting gears to accelerate ever more, but no one is steering.

What the structure of modern science, which gives man ever increasing power to control his existence, demands is precisely a social value-orientation. The adding of partial rationalities to one another does not automatically guarantee that the whole will be harmonious. On the contrary, if there is no orientation through an overarching total view, the irrationality of the whole can only become greater. Modern society blindly races on. While the rationality of the means is rapidly increasing, that of the goals is quickly diminishing.[12]

Utopian thinking is born from need. If science progresses without a utopian picture of the future, human life in society becomes more disoriented. The attention which philosophers, scientists and politicians have shown for utopian thinking in the past decade, thus turns out to be the result of a necessity. Riesman views the revival of utopian thinking as one of the most important intellectual duties of our time. "Utopia," he pointedly says, "is time located in the future: it is a social order which has not yet been tried, though it is a realistic possibility, not a mere idle dream."[13] Polak, Picht,[14] Mead,[15] Klages, Van Steenbergen[16] and others recognize the catalyzing effect of utopian visions with respect to social progress. The synthesizing and exemplary models of the future help society to raise the problem of choice between different possibilities of development in a responsible and critical fashion and facilitate the quest for a solution.

The utopian intention of these authors appears to be well-balanced. They do not simply intend to extend the existing lines of development into the future. They ascribe a fundamental importance to the dimension of creative imagination which envisages qualitatively different possibilities. On the other hand, they do not overindulge in an exotic nostalgia for unlimited horizons and emphasize that the utopian picture of the future has an experimental-empirical character. For example, Picht pictures the future as a combination of prognosis, utopia and planning. The prognosis represents the experimental-empirical aspect, it makes a scientific diagnosis of the future, formulates a number of alternative possibilities and indicates different directions on the basis of the information supplied by the existing situation. From these materials the utopian imagination then creatively builds the optimum picture of the future. In this way social imagination creates new possibilities, without running wild. The third element, planning, sees to it that the utopically created picture of the future is realized.[17] Klages pleads for a projective sociology. He rejects the neo-positivistic trend of Max Weber, the structural functionalism of Parsons and the evolution according to the laws of history on which, he says, dialectical sociology is based. Describing sociology as the zone in between reality and possibility, Klages wants scientific rationality in the investigation of the future to be enlarged in the direction of the imagination and concrete utopia.[18]

The neo-Marxist trend, mentioned in the Introduction, occupies a special place in contemporary utopian thinking. The central position in this trend is occupied by the concept of alienation and history is viewed as dialectical progress. Neo-Marxism wants to demolish the petrified Marxist structure and start afresh with the explanation of history through internal dialectics. It points out that the existing social order represses many desires, wishes and potentials. It wishes to make people conscious of this repression and thus create liberating elbowroom for that which has not yet reached consciousness and has not yet come to be. The concrete utopia, moreover, fulfills a psychoanalytic function because it brings the repressed possibilities to the surface. Against Marx, neo-Marxist writers, such as Bloch, Adorno,[19] Kolakowski, Kofler and Marcuse, defend the critico-dynamic role of utopian thinking. The concrete utopia, on the one hand, fosters the active negation or negative dialectics with respect to the existing situation; on the other, it constructively transcends this negation. That's why Kolakowski says: "But the Left will never accept the reproach that it is only negative, for every constructive program is a negation, and vice versa. Without a constructive program the Left would not have a negative program either since the two expressions refer to one and the same. . . . The Left thus is characterized by negation *but not by negation alone*; on the contrary, the Left is characterized by the direction of this negation, that is to say, by its *utopia*."[20]

The neo-Marxist utopian thinkers attempt to make a synthesis between the Marxist theory of alienation and the Freudian doctrine of repression. While Freud usually equates culture with repression, the modern utopians of the Hegelian-Marxist trend think that the coming civilization with its technico-economic development offers the possibility of doing away with repression. The old desire for a paradise finds its modern translation in such expressions as "society without violence," "the reign of freedom," "pacified existence" and a "fatherless society."

In Kofler's book *The Ascetical Eros* the term "ascetical" refers to the performance principle and "eros" to the pleasure principle. Kofler sees classless society as a harmonious reunion of the Dionysian and the Apollonian. His book clearly shows a nostalgia for reconciliation on a higher level of the original primitive condition in which work and playful enjoyment were not yet distinct. Marcuse speaks about "the end of Utopia," because the so-called utopian possibilities are no longer utopian but already constitute the historico-social negation of the existing situation. The wish to relegate these real possibilities to the "no man's land" of Utopia is, according to him, a result of the ideological alienation of the performance principle.[21] Kolakowski shows a greater sense of relativity when he expresses the value of the utopian imagination in these words: "The existence of the utopia as utopia is the undeniable condition for the possibility that the utopia may cease to be utopia."[22] This neo-Marxist trend tries to raise the synthesis between part and whole, between individual and "species," to a higher level by means of the utopia, to which it also ascribes a psychoanalytic and socioanalytic function.

5. THE ESSENTIAL CHARACTERISTICS OF THE UTOPIA

The term "utopia" has become very fashionable today. But one who tries accurately to determine what the term means finds different descriptions. Some people view utopias as unreal wishful dreams and an innocent pastime; others regard them as dangerous and tyrannical hallucinations; and others, again, look at them as catalyzers of human progress. The reason for this divergence of opinion lies, I think, in an inaccurate use of the phenomenological reduction, one which prematurely stops with the external side of a particular phenomenon.[1]

Generally speaking, three variations can be distinguished in the definitions of the utopia. The first conceives the utopia as a particular literary style and seeks the distinguishing characteristic of it in certain literary qualities. The second calls the utopia a "utopian," i.e., naive and prescientific, way of thinking about society. The third identifies the utopia with the critical approach to the form man has given to society.[2]

If the sequence of these three classifications is compared with the development of utopian thinking in European culture, one can notice that it runs parallel to a similar historical development. The first definition, which starts with the literary style of the novel, corresponds to the bloom of utopian writings during the Renaissance. The definition fits the style of More's *Utopia*, Campanella's *City of the Sun* and Bacon's *Novum Organon* and *Nova Atlantis*. These writings reflect the era of the Renaissance, when man began to believe in his own power and the positive sciences slowly began to flourish. A desire arose then to change the world, but matters did not yet go beyond a mere desire. It remained a dreaming about a more perfect world. This wishful dreaming found its expression in the utopian novels which fictitiously and idyllically painted conditions of perfect happiness. The playfully fictitious character of these utopian novels easily makes one seek the criterion of utopian writing in nothing but literary qualities.

As Bloch points out, it is wrong to limit the utopian intention to Thomas More's approach. One might as well claim that electricity should be reduced to amber because the ancient Greeks first discovered the phenomenon of electricity in this stone—the term "electricity" is derived from *electron*, the Greek word for amber.[3] Nevertheless, More's *Utopia* is not a purely literary novel. The utopian intention plays an implicit role in it as criticizing the evil conditions then existing and thus attempting to overcome the imperfections of society. In the utopian novels of the Renaissance the form and intention of utopian writing still remain undistinguished from each other, which means that the literary form can easily mask the implicit utopian intention.

The second description, which looks at the utopia as a prescientific way of thinking, is based on the scientistic ideal of science, which rapidly began to gain ground after the eighteenth century. For the optimism of the eighteen century utopia and reason could still go hand in hand in a "natural" fashion because of the prevailing belief in homogeneous and continuous progress. But the rise of positivism overemphasized the value of science at the expense of utopian thinking. The consequences of this were that, on the one hand, the utopian approach was reduced to a prescientific way of thinking and, on the other, that reason increasingly assumed the form of a narrow and functional rationality.

The title of one of Friedrich Engels's works is significant in this respect. He called it: *The Development of Socialism from Utopia to Science.* Marx and Engels use the word "utopia" to refer to what they call the utopian socialism of Saint-Simon, Fourier, Cabet, Owen and others. They call these men "utopians" because, interested as they are in the social ideal, they still try to explain history too much in terms of abstract ideas and ideals. But they could hardly have done otherwise, say Marx and Engels, because in their time capitalism had not yet sufficiently developed to discover the laws governing it. That's why those socialists had to speak about the development of society in a utopian fashion. But Marx and Engels thought that the time had come to replace that utopian socialism with their own scientific socialism.

When the science of sociology arose, the utopian way of looking at things was viewed as a substitute for the still defective scientific analysis of social phenomena. Classical Marxism and the new bourgeois sociology characterized the utopian visions as interesting from the standpoint of literature but otherwise merely prescientific forerunners of true science. In Mannheim's words, incipient sociology looked as the utopias as "a substitute for the scientific analysis of social phenomena."[4]

The following development can thus be noted. In the first variation of utopia, form and intention still remain more or less indistinct, but in the second variation the critical intention already occupies a more prominent position. The critical intention *per se* belongs to science but, for the time being, this intention manifests itself in the utopian form. The utopia, then, is important not so much as a literary genre but as a utopian—that is to say, still naive and prescientific—expression of the critical intention.

The transition to the third variation should be easy to understand now. Not the form but the intention consititutes the essence of the utopia here. When in the course of the twentieth century the bourgeois social science had declared the existing society the only conceivable one and not subject to further perfection, there was no longer any need for utopian thinking. Thus Lalande still describes the utopia as "an attractive but unrealizable political or social ideal in which real facts, human nature and the conditions of existence are not taken into account."[5] Today, however, we assume a more critical attitude with respect to the existing social structures and we see that precisely the utopian intention constitutes the critical ferment of social development. Not the literary form but the soberly expressed critical portrayal of the future is the essence of the utopia. Socio-critical science is identical with utopian-inspired science. Strange as it seems, precisely such neo-Marxist writers as Horkheimer and Bloch turn out to be the forerunners in the revaluation of the utopian function. Marx and traditional Marxism, it should be recalled, had little respect for the ideal and moral power of the utopia. But in the 1930s Horkheimer and Bloch already spoke about the "concrete utopia of Marxism."

The critical intention to break through the existing conditions and achieve a better future turn out to be the essence of the utopian phenomenon. In the literary view of utopia during the Renaissance this intention was already present but only implicitly; Marx and the incipient bourgeois sociology described this intention as naive and in this sense utopian, but today its value for producing a change in society receives great emphasis. The controversy about utopia changes from the scientific question as to which phenomenon is represented by the term "utopia" to the moral question about the value to be attached to the utopian intention.[6] The utopian critique, which places itself at a distance from actual conditions, and the utopian imagination, which starts from the assumption that "things could have been different," turn out to be increasingly more necessary for a fruitful pursuit of science.

The essence of the utopia consists in the liberating impetus to transcend the limitations of human existence in the direction of a better future. The utopia fulfills a critical function. It presents a concrete picture of the ideal and thus exercises a constant moral pressure on society to bring about a better world. Every utopia, which wishes to open new perspectives for society, at the same time assumes a negative attitude toward the existing situation which it endeavors to change. This means that the utopian intention is both explorative and normative; it offers both a destructive image of the present and a constructive image of the future. It provides man with a horizon within which he can breathe and realize his freedom. In the following chapters we will examine all these utopian elements more closely.

6. THE FUNDAMENTAL UTOPIAN DIALECTICS

As we will see more in detail later, every concrete utopia places itself at a distance (negation) from the existing situation (affirmation) and is directed toward a better future (negation of the negation). This concrete utopian triad is the phenomenal form of an all-encompassing utopian process. This total process is, as it were, the background against which every concrete utopian event takes place. This transcendental[1] utopian field of vision is *a priori* normative both for the manner in which observable reality appears to us and for the manner in which we deal with this reality. The fundamental pattern of the utopia is transcendental in the sense that, on the one hand, it doesn't coincide with every concrete utopia, and on the other, doesn't exist independently of the concrete utopia in the manner of an objective datum. The fundamental utopia doesn't coincide with the concrete utopia but is precisely the transcendental ground from which we start in any concrete portrayal of the future. The fundamental utopian pattern is not itself immediately given and directly visible, but it is included in, and indirectly visible through the utopian interpretations which we make. The expression "transcendental utopian orientation" doesn't refer to something beyond man's reach, nor to something within his reach, but indicates this reach itself from which we have already started.

The utopian presupposition from which all concrete utopian thinking starts, the archtypical basic structures of every concrete utopian desire, the "circle of circles," constitute the trinity of paradise, fall and salvation or, in more secularized language, the dialectical triad of thesis (affirmation), antithesis (negation) and synthesis (negation of the negation).

The thesis is the first phase of mankind. It is the period when people are still preconsciously united with one another and with nature in a naively unquestioned immediacy. The story of Paradise presents a picture of this condition. In the Garden of Eden man lives in perfect harmony with nature and himself. This phase, which Hegel calls the "in itself" is one of preconscious immediacy. The antithesis arises because man becomes conscious of himself. Imagination, reason and self-consciousness disrupt the primordial harmony. Mankind becomes particularized in individuals. At the moment when man arrives at individual consciousness with its knowledge of good and evil, he also becomes "schismatic," he separates himself from the rest. The evolution of consciousness is accompanied by the loss of the paradiselike harmony.

The original immediacy and bond have changed into a division between subject and object, between individual and society. Man as individualized consciousness knows—or rather *is*—the opposition between inner and outer, the internal world and the external world. Individual consciousness, which Hegel calls the "for itself," is a "false" consciousness because of its separation. But it is impossible to return to the prehuman paradiselike condition. Man must go forward to build a dwelling place for himself by humanizing the world and humanizing himself. That's why people try to bring about the synthesis between subject and object, the reunion of individual and society, on a higher level through "mediation."

Man is on the way; he is between the "no longer" of the distant past and the "not yet" of the distant future. Thus he experiences two contradictory orientations. On the one hand, he knows anxiety through the loss of the protective security he used to have; on the other, he has the courage to go beyond the past of secure unfreedom to the future of free humanity. He is nostalgic for the protective custody of the maternal womb and of nature, but he also wishes to escape this all-powerful womb and himself achieve his freedom in a courageous adventure.

The history of both individual and mankind shows that the progressive tendency usually prevails over its regressive counterpart. Mankind plunges into an adventure and goes beyond one boundary after the other in the hope of building up a new and better existence. It continues to hope for unity and the reconciliation of freedom and order, for the conscious and free harmony of everyone with everything, of the individual with the universal. Hegel especially believed in the concretely universal as the sythesis of the abstract universality of the "in itself" and the particularization of the "for itself." The concretely universal is the transcendence of every opposition between the self-realization of the individual and that of the totality.

Every concrete utopian transcendence of the existing situation in the direction of a better future is nourished by this utopian nostalgia which lies behind it. In the utopias from Plato to Thomas More, from Owen to Wells the memory of a paradiselike condition in the very distant past is unconsciously present. Precisely the nostalgia for the lost innocence of primordial existence accompanies the utopian hope for a new and better life. The utopian man is afflicted by the memory of the lost paradise of security; that's why he ventures forward and dreams about a new life, an unstructured existence on a higher level. Although the utopian imagination wishes to offer man a realistic alternative to the existing situation, without getting lost in things infinitely distant, its hope for limited historical progress and improvement is inspired by the dream of utopian happiness. Especially the utopian writers of the Renaissance, who knew man's desire to take his destiny into his own hands but who were still frustrated by their technical powerlessness to bring about the realization of their dreams, spent their time in wishful dreaming about a peaceful state of happiness.

Two tendencies are always found in the idyllic portrayal of a perfect happiness in which things now still antagonistic blend into harmony.[2] One tendency puts greater emphasis on sensuous delight or harmony with nature. The utopian searchers of happiness dream of a new earthly paradise, in which an authentic freedom reigns and happiness is sought in unbridled sensuous delight. The utopian story plays here with the idea of a paradise of sense enjoyment. The other tendency seeks to attain salvation by means of law and order. It expects happiness in an earthly state in which everything is governed by careful planning and in a collectivistic fashion. Most utopian writings, however, such as those of More and Campanella, try to combine both tendencies.

The modern utopia also is, on the one hand, driven by a nostalgic desire for a paradise lost in the past, but on the other, it dreams about an ideal picture of harmony and reconciliation in the future. The modern utopia, however, in contrast with older utopias proposes or posits the future less absolutely. It strives to attain a judicious combination of imagination and scientific knowledge. Its ideal remains the receding horizon of endless progress.

A special place is occupied in today's utopian thinking by the new Marxist trend because it very strongly emphasizes the ideal of unity and reconciliation. The classical utopian tendencies toward the paradise of sensuous delight and the state of happiness find here their modern equivalent in the Freudian distinction between the pleasure principle and the performance principle or the principle of reality. In imitation of Nietzsche, others, such as Kofler, refer to the Dionysian and the Apollonian elements. Dionysius, as the carefree and exuberant god of the wine, symbolizes sensuous delight and intoxication, while Apollo, as the severe and grave god of the sun, is the symbol of order and thoughtfulness.

According to Freud, eros always continues to live in a state of antagonism with the principle of reality, but Kofler thinks that a growing reconciliation is becoming possible. Kofler is guided in this by the utopia, which he describes as "the dialectical unity of the achieving-Apollinian man and the lusting-Dionysian man, or the "playful" man, i.e., the man who erotically delights in creative achievement, and the man who actively realizes himself in delight."[3] Kofler thinks that the realization of this goal implies an even more profound historical break than the transition from primordial times to the class society. Nevertheless, he doesn't wish to speak at once of an eschatological final goal. He characterizes his utopia as a "relative absolute," by which he means that, although the ultimate goal comes toward man as something absolute in history, it nevertheless is striven for by man himself in an endlessly relative way.[4] According to Kofler, the utopia is a concept which dialectically unites relativity and absoluteness. In spite of a certain feeling for relativity, Kofler expects that the third and definitive phase of mankind's history is approaching as a possibility.

The tripartite division of mankind's history and that of the world receives even greater emphasis in Marcuse than in Kofler. Marcuse also has a greater expectation of salvation. He wishes to believe that the total emancipation of nature and history is close at hand. That's why he holds that "the end of utopia" is possible. His triple division of history is as follows. The first phase of "the lost time," the paradise of the past, must again be brought to consciousness through psychoanalytical memory (anamnesis). The second phase is that of the socio-economic order in which production is internally connected with repression. But this second period has now reached the critical point at which a revolutionary turn to the third and definitive phase is at hand. The critical memory of the better past and the critical cognitive phantasy of the better future make a radical break in history possible. When the alienation of the intermediary period will be dissolved in a total emancipation, the third and definitive phase of mankind's history will have started.

Not all neo-Marxists equally emphasize this background dialectics of the utopia. Bloch turns away from pictures of the future which make the transcendental presupposition the very content of all concrete-utopian thought. He calls this "sheer 'utopizing.' " Such portrayals of the future dissolve in what he calls "*abstract* utopias."[5] The *concrete* utopia, on the other hand, creates wishful portrayals of the future which offer a realistically possible goal and indicates ways of reaching it. This concrete expectation of the future, however, is still grounded in the utopian principle of the "no longer" of the paradise lost and the "not yet" of the recovered fatherland of self-identity. This primordial desire is the source from which everything comes forth, but the concrete utopia articulates and realizes this desire in the space-time of history. The realistic utopian picture of the future, on the one hand, doesn't positivistically cling to what actually exists in its immediate visibility but, on the other, it doesn't evaoporate into the claim that this or that future with its mythological invisibility will "actually" come about. The utopian function knows a "transcending without transcendence."[6]

7. THE CONCRETE UTOPIA

The leading writer of the utopian genre is, of course, Thomas More, who began his *Utopia* with a critical analysis of the ailments afflicting Europe, and in particular England, in his time. He put himself at a distance from the reality existing in his days; he "negated" that which was "affirmed" as a fact in perceptible reality. The second part of More's *Utopia* contains the portrayal of the better future, the "negation of the negation." This is the dialectical method of the utopian intention, which corresponds to the dialectical development of human and societal reality.

Man dwells actively in the world. He dialectically moves between possibility and facticity, originality and reliance on what is already, the creation of new meaning and the acceptance of established meanings. Man constitutes the world and this world is essentially *unfinished*. The reality in which man lives and which he constitutes is a meaningful reality, that is to say, it contains a direction, moves toward a better future. That's why Bloch says that "that which is can be not true."[1] And Marcuse remarks: "Facts are facts only if related to that which is not yet fact and yet manifests itself in the given facts as a real possibility. Or, facts are what they are only as moments in a process that leads beyond them to that which is not yet fulfilled in fact."[2] In the light of a better future, the critical observer will therefore judge that which *de facto* is as something unfinished. He analyzes existing reality in reference to the "not yet" of the normative future.

Mankind lives in the antithesis of the "split," the duality of subject and object, of freedom and necessity, of individual and species. It tries to reconcile the contrary poles by establishing "intermediaries," means between the opposites. Man creates means to bridge the distance separating the inner and the outer world.

The term "means" should be broadly understood here. It refers not only to material means, such as tools and machines, not only to social organs and institutes, but also to patterns of conduct and normative objectifications. All these objectifications come about through the dialectical movement between subject and nature. In this sense man is at the same time both *homo faber* and *homo fabricatus*, the man who makes and the man who is made.

The development process of creating means, however, is in constant danger of stagnation. We are touching here the core of the phenomenon of dialectical alienation. The means, which should fulfill the function of intermediary and of reconciling the opposite poles, have a tendency to become autonomous. That's why Nietzsche already spoke of a "revolt of the means." The intermediary must always try to make himself superfluous, but he tends to maintain the division in order to maintain himself. When this happens, the means block the road to the goals and themselves become goals. Marxism speaks here of the fetishism of "reification" which is an obstacle to the development of history.

Creative man constantly transforms the natural world into a world of culture. But objectified culture—objective spirit in the sense of Hegel—which in a certain phase has been projected by man's freedom turns against this freedom in a different phase of history. Constituting man is in danger of becoming one-sidedly constituted man, *homo faber* becomes *homo fabricatus*. Constituted reality, which should be a disposition for a new human project, now begins to restrict man's freedom itself. Man who began as master of his order now becomes its servant. The society which at first let its idealistic impetus crystallize in norms and patterns of conduct now proceeds to adore its own creations in a dogmatic and ideological attitude. Society becomes entangled in its own products and constitutions. It lives, in Sartre's language, under the pressure of the practico-inert field, it suffers from the structural violence of inertia.

Man, however, is essentially a "movement of transcendence." He doesn't coincide with himself, as he did in the "thesis" of the preconscious phase, he no longer possesses the sense life of the animal, which is at rest in what it *is* and is encompassed by its life situations. Conscious man stands between possibility and facticity, between aspiration and boundaries, between a plurality of meaning and a univocal existence. He constantly wants to resolve existing reality into new possibilities. Human freedom over and over again tries to transcend one-dimensional facticities, it wants to melt the ice of the constituted and change it into a flowing source of new constituting givings of meaning.

History is full of critical periods in which the tension between the possible and the actual becomes too great. There are times when the house that has been built becomes unsatisfactory and is even beyond remodeling. The existing structures of society have become petrified and obstruct the breakthrough toward a new future. When this happens the idealists put themselves in opposition to the realists and begin to speak a different language. The realists appeal to the established law and order and speak of the "normative power of what *de facto* is." They approach the possible from the actual and think in terms of a gradual evolution. The idealists, however, believe in man as a "being of possibilities" and want to deduce another factual situation from the ideal possibility. They think in terms of a radical revolution. When a society exists in a phase of qualitative change, it finds itself in a critical situation.

Such a fundamental crisis causes a vacuum. Man is fearful of any forward step, for it means giving up a familiar situation in exchange for one that is unfamilar. But having to cross the threshold toward a new perspective and entering an area where there are as yet only possibilities is something that scares most people to death. They see themselves caught, as it were, between the devil and the deep blue sea. The old familiar conditions are no longer viable, and the new and unfamilar conditions offer as yet nothing to hold on to. Scared by such a vacuum, a society can desperately try to cling to the past; it can also prematurely fill the new conditions with dogmatic pseudo-certainties. In both cases it is governed by fear and seeks refuge in a pseudo-security. Only the utopian-minded man dares to undertake the existential adventure. He has the courage to disregard his anxiety and to cross the threshold toward a new perspective; and he will gropingly give shape to this new field of presence.

The utopian man loves the strange and the new. He will not give in to the defense-mechanism of projection and he will not fill the heuristic vacuum with pseudo-certainties. The utopian man is characterized by an open mentality. He dares to look at the phenomena of society in a new perspective. On the other hand, he has a sense of relativity. He realizes that the new perspective constantly needs to be corrected by what is happening in society. The utopian truth is fundamentally revolutionary, but its revolutionary character need not per se be identified with violence. For the revolutionary force of the utopia lies mainly in its spiritual power, the power of a new idea. It is possible that a revolutionary change must sometimes be brought about by physical violence, but in such a case the revolution is only partly successful. Any violent revolution is an historical event that has not yet succeeded in being itself, since the aim of every revolution is to bring about more freedom and peace. A radically humanizing revolution, if it doesn't wish to tread on its own goals, must be nourished by the moral force of the utopia. The most powerful and indeed the only weapon to bring about greater humanity is the spiritual weapon of the utopia. By its faith in the power of its own spirit, the utopia makes society ripe for a fundamental change.

8. UTOPIA AND MYTH

The distinction between utopia and myth is rather strange. Two strategic fronts delineate themselves in this distinction. The first lies between the ancient myth and the utopia, the other between the utopia and the modern society myth. The utopia thus lies between two lines of battle. On the rear, it must rid itself of a mythical past in which man's destiny and the order of the world are immutably determined from the beginning to the end. At the front, it must safeguard itself against a mythical future, in which human history is determined from an immutable standpoint. In the one case the beginning and in the other the end threatens the life force of the utopia.

Let us begin with a consideration of the relationship between the ancient myth of the pristine beginning and the utopia. In scholarly literature the myth turns out to be almost intangible and subject to all kinds of interpretation. Without delving too deeply into the much-disputed concept of "myth," we may be able to sketch a few distinguishing characteristics of mythical consciousness in opposition to utopian consciousness. Utopian thinking has always been fundamentally a movement of emancipation. This tendency was already present in the ancient utopias, such as that of Plato. The utopia causes a Copernican revolution in the picture of the future. The myth, on the other hand, gives meaning to the present on the basis of a primordial event. Where mythical consciousness prevails, the utopian intention cannot flourish. The myth believes in the immutable destiny of things, but the utopia starts with a changeable order.

That's why there is a clear-cut distinction between myth and utopia. The mythical story wishes to depict the pristine event which occurred outside human history. The myth describes things which unconditionally apply to man and which he simply has to accept. Salvation or final catastrophe come to him from without and from above. The myth describes a sacral plan of the world, one which falls upon man as a grace or a fate and which he undergoes. The myth expresses a divine decree which vertically enters the world and determines man.

In the utopia, however, man himself goes forward. He himself wants to overcome the limitations of his existence and go in search of happiness. While in the myth the new and the alien come to man, in the utopia man himself tries to explore the new and the alien. The utopian horizon breaks open the narrow boundaries of existence and entices man to leave his fixed dwelling place. The myth makes man stand in adoration before the sacred and the immutable, but the utopia makes him an adventurer who sets out for distant and unknown lands.

The myth expresses but the utopia invents.[1] The myth depicts the overarching eternity in the form of a historical narrative, but the utopia works in the opposite direction and wishes to attain the eternal by way of human history. The myth starts with the gods in order to reach man, but the utopia starts with man in order to reach the level of the gods. The myth is directed to "the eternal man," but the utopia to "the evolving man." In the mythical attitude of life human history is seen from the *archē*, the origin, but in the utopian perspective human existence is viewed in the light of the future. While in the myth suprahistorical salvation determines the "somewhere" of man, the utopian "nowhere" is conceived as a transcendence of the human "somewhere." The mythical consciousness breathes the atmosphere of necessity and immutability, but the utopian consciousness is characterized by a spirit of freedom and changeability.

In the historical survey of utopian thought we have seen how this movement of emancipation has gradually taken place. At first, the utopia was limited to conceptions of the world fashioned on a divine world plan or a natural cosmic order. Myth and utopia were still closely connected. But with the Enlightenment man becomes more independent, more self-reliant and more critical. He liberates himself from supra-earthly powers, thus acquiring the freedom to make his own life. The future lies unfixed before him.

But while Western society has thus liberated itself from the old mythical consciousness, its freedom is now endangered by the modern phenomenon of the social myth. Many people are scared and hesitate before the openness of the future. A vacuum arises which needs to be filled. The social myths respond to this need for security and anchorage. The anxiety for the new and the unknown, spoken of in the preceding chapter, can easily make a society resort to the security of dogmatic totalitarian portrayals of the future. Because they are unable to bear unclear and uncertain situations, many people escape from their unbearable sense of powerlessness by taking refuge in expectations of deliverance.

Sorel was the man who connected the concept "myth" with certain social and political aims. He distinguished the social myth from the social utopia. According to him, the social myth, unlike the utopia, is not an intellectual thought-construct but a spontaneous and emotional product. The social myth, he says, should not be scrutinized for its truth value but should be used as a means to stir up the masses. Rational truth, he holds, does not set the masses into motion; that's why it is better to use irrational and mythical emotions.

The difference between the social utopia and the social myth should be immediately evident. The social utopia seeks to build up a picture of the future in the light of which one can look critically at the existing society and improve it. Reason and emotion are attuned to each other in the utopia. Within the framework of human and rational possibilities it pleads for a better future. The social myth, on the other hand, has psychotic overtones. Human reason is dragged along by uncontrolled emotions. The protrayal of the future has the features of a hallucinatory salvation and wishes to lib-

erate the masses of their burden of freedom. Concrete social and
political aims are clothed in the mythical garment of absoluteness.
Social myths, such as those of Fascism and Nazism, demand a blind
belief in, and a total surrender to their prophetic expectations of
salvation. Society thus lives under the tyranny of its own portrayal
of the future.[2]

The social myth possesses a totalitarian and authoritarian character, it is a projection of a consciousness suffering from nervous
exhaustion. The man who creates such a myth wishes to reestablish
control over his feelings of anxiety and uneasiness by means the defense-mechanism of projection. He projects an ideal of perfection
outside himself, makes it independent of himself and personifies it
as something superior to himself, and then sacrifices his own human
autonomy to it. The mythical picture of the future is essentially a
regression to the primitive phase of undifferentiated existence, to
the womb of nature, i.e., the phase before man became free. The
new ideal which is absolutized is actually always a repetition of the
old myth. All the characteristics of the ancient myth reappear in it.
The mythical element, however, is more difficult to recognize in the
social myth. The reason is, on the one hand, that the social myth
claims to refer to the socio-political order and, on the other, that it
camouflages its irrational character through the alienating effect of
psychological rationalization.[3]

The social myth camouflages itself by its quasi-rationality and its
quasi-portrayal of the future. That's why writers like Karl Popper[4]
and H. Albert[5] vehemently object to the utopia. They think that
every totalitarian regime is a realized utopia and that every utopia
is a plan for establishing a totalitarian regime. Popper, for example,
conceives utopian rationalism as a masochistic suicide of human
reason and declares that, no matter how benevolent utopian aims
are, they do not bring happiness but only the familiar misery of
being condemned to live under tyranny.

Popper's defense of democracy may be laudable and one may
commend him for drawing attention to the danger of totalitarianism, but in my opinion he misinterprets the social facts. His identification of the totalitarian myth with the utopia is based on a mis-

taken analogy of the quasi-rationality and the quasi-picture of the future presented by the myth with the genuine rationality and the genuine picture of the future offered by the utopia. Obviously we are not merely arguing here about words and definitions, in the sense that what one calls a social myth the other prefers to call a social utopia. What is at stake here is a different interpretation of the sociological phenomena, a difference that finds expression in the distinction between social myth and social utopia. The crucial point is that in our society utopias do not give rise to totalitarianism, but rather the absence of a sound vision of the future causes this void to be filled by the totalitarianism of social myths.

Through the utopia, society gives itself a perspective on the future. The utopian horizon is the "translation" of what mankind anticipates. This horizon offers society an *open anchorage* in the distance by its constructive project. When this is not done, the open space becomes an *empty void* which causes a panic fear. In this panic two escape routes are available. Society can fearfully cling to the existing situation and aggressively fight anything new; it then takes refuge in the *status quo*. Or it can blindly plunge into the empty void, fleeing from the existing world into the hallucinatory world of fancies. In either case man and society become self-estranged. In the one situation the existing order exercises an authoritarian rule, in the other the same is done by the hallucinating fancies about the future. These two extreme attitudes evoke one another. In its anxiety and fear of the empty void, society is driven to and fro between them.

Human freedom can flourish only within the framework of a horizon of the future that is a meaningful projection. Freedom lives in between openness and restriction, it demands the absence of compulsion but also the presence of support. When freedom is too much restricted by the existing conditions, man is, as it were, imprisoned. An overstructured situation offers no perspective, it leaves man the "freedom" of a prisoner in his chains. On the other hand, when man finds himself in a totally open condition without any anchorage or support, he lives in an arid desert. Then, too, he is seized by fear and anxiety, caught as he is by the total openness of the void. He then is a prisoner of his freedom because his situation is too unstructured. Total restriction deprives man of all possibilities of freedom and destroys his humanity, but total openness dissolves his freedom into thin air and makes existence impossible. The optimal leeway for the blossoming of freedom is present when the existing situation is no longer experienced as merely restrictive. Rather a horizon of possibilities has been projected and this horizon is not experienced as "sheer emptiness" because it retains its bonds with reality.

Now it is the utopia which guarantees this optimal leeway for man's self-realization. Its vision sets the existing situation in motion and offers society a perspective on the future. The established structures, which permit only the freedom a prisoner enjoys in his chains, are broken open. On the other hand, the utopia sees to it that the future is not sought independently of empirical reality. The utopia doesn't wish to evaporate into thin air, thus letting society become the prisoner of its own freedom. The utopia has a "mediated" openness because of its ambivalent character: it is both something distant and a horizon. It is a projected stage in the development of society toward the future. The dominant note of the utopian mood lies precisely in its sensitivity to relativity; it objects to absolutizing either the past or the present.

It is no coincidence that the rise of industrial civilization took place at the same time as the birth of social myths. Modern technological power forces man to assume responsibility for his own destiny. The tempestuous evolution in industry automatically orientates society to the future. Not the past but only the future can be the norm. The familiar religious worldview and picture of man has lost credence, but faith in new values which give direction to the future is still missing. Thus a nihilistic sense of life reigns in our time with its lack of perspective. Moreover, positivism and capitalism have levelled life to a single dimension by evaluating everything and everyone one-sidedly in terms of usefulness. When everything and everyone is approached in a thinglike fashion, man's inner life remains infantile. Thus the technocratic society finds itself in a precarious situation. On the one hand, it is the prisoner of its own freedom since it has no possibility of identifying with spiritual values which give meaning and direction to life. On the other, the technocratic and bureaucratic order is a golden cage, which offers society only the freedom allotted to a prisoner.

One can readily understand that in this situation of despair our century is prone to resort to the doubtful remedy of the social myth. The mythical portrayal of the future is the embodiment and the personification of the frustrated desire for humanity and freedom. Such a myth seemingly gives society a possibility of identification and liberation. With its expectation of salvation, the social myth acts as a soothing remedy against the painful straits of the present situation and it fills the frightening void of the future with absolutized certainties which allow no openness whatsoever.

Popper rightly emphasizes the danger that our society will lapse into totalitarianism. In reaction to this, he is a protagonist of what he calls "critical rationalism." He pleads for a kind of social engineering, an *ad hoc* technique, which improves society step by step. However, the question still remains: which picture of the future offers guidance in this step by step progress?[6] It is precisely the absence of a guiding norm which makes our society so vulnerable to totalitarian myths. Popper opposes historicism, which holds that society is governed by ironclad laws of history, so that the future is predictable. But Popper incorrectly confuses such a social-mythical picture of the future with that of the utopia.

The utopia is not a dogmatic and prophetic representation of the future, but an inspiring force because it views the future as a free human task. Undoubtedly, the utopia is nourished by the "eternal" ideals of total peace and total brotherhood. Precisely for this reason, however, it will never conceive any concrete portrayal of the future as "the reign of freedom," but always only as a provisional reign, a reign that is never yet the final one. The concrete utopia wants to go forward and desires a better future, but it doesn't claim to bring this future to its final completion. As Bloch succinctly expresses its character at the end of his major work, "The conscience of the concrete utopia certainly does not positivistically cling to the fact of *immediate visibility*, but even more certainly it doesn't evaporate into absolutizing pure *mythological invisibility* into a fact."[7]

9. UTOPIA AND IDEOLOGY

There is even more controversy about the meaning of the term "ideology" than there is about that of "utopia." Three different ways of conceiving ideology prevail in our time.[1] First of all, there is the positive view, in which the ideology is described as a more or less well-rounded system of ideas and tendencies governing socio-political action. Secondly, there is the negative view, which can have two different overtones. One ascribes to the ideology ignorance of the world as it really is. In this way a distinction is sometimes made between a pragmatic or realistic approach and an ideological approach. The other variation places even more emphasis on the negative aspect, it equates ideologly with dishonesty and a lack of sincerity. Ideologies thus are pseudo-ideas and descriptive rationalizations to justify and defend the material interest of a particular group or class. All of these three contemporary variations have their historical roots in the past.

It was only at a relatively recent date that attention began to be paid to the question of the critique of ideology and the ideological consciousness which makes people adhere to certain ideas and determined by them. The question of the origin, the validity and tenability of such ideas arose only in the Modern Age. In a closed and static society, based on traditional and securely anchored values, the necessary elbowroom for critique is lacking. This explains why the first reflections on such ideas arose only after the Middle Ages at the time of the Renaissance.

The Greco-Roman and the medieval periods held a cosmological worldview. The cosmic order with its ideas and laws, accepted on either metaphysical or religious grounds, externally and vertically determined man and society. But with the Renaissance a Copernican revolution occurred in man's experience of existence. The end of the Middle Ages and the beginning of the Modern Age can be characterized as follows. Man gives up his cosmic view of the world and of himself, he becomes conscious of his own power and thus also of himself. He tries to liberate himself of the theological and metaphysical presuppositions of the old view and to assume at least a critical attitude in its respect. In this way there slowly arises the problem of the ideology and of the ideological consciousness. Two factors are mainly responsible for the rise of this problem, viz., the birth of individualism and that of rationalism, which aims at knowledge of empirical facts. The growing individualism makes people assume a more independent attitude with respect to the ideas prevalent in the group, and rationalism makes European thinkers refuse to indulge in sheer speculation or to start from *a priori* religious assumptions.

The epistemological revolution was mainly brought about by Descrates, Francis Bacon and Locke. But this should not be taken to mean that every theological and metaphysical justification of life, and consequently also of knowledge, was at once rejected. For example, Descartes sought the origin of ideas in the human subject himself and no longer, as Plato had done, in a transcendent world of ideas, but these ideas in man still had their source in God. The most important man of this period with respect to the problem of ideology was Francis Bacon. He was less inclined to Cartesian immanence and investigated how the subject can approach nature with the fewest possible prejudices. He explored the "idols," the prejudices of human knowledge.

This critical approach to ideas and prejudices was taken over by the Enlightenment in the eighteenth century. The very term "ideology" dates from this time and was introduced by Destutt de Tracy. Following the line of the French Encyclopedists, such as Condillac, Tracy tried to formulate a "science of ideas," an "ideology," which should be the foundation of the sciences. Our knowledge thus should lay bare the laws or ideas of nature and reject all elements which obstruct the viewing of this reality. The principal obstacle to be removed, he held, is the authoritarian "priestly deception." Tracy's "science of ideas" has nothing except the name in common with Plato's doctrine of ideas. Ideas are no longer independent, suprahuman entities in the form of archetypes or exemplars. As contents of consciousness, they are reduced to experiences caused in consciousness by the external world. Nothing remains here either of Descartes' innate ideas. Although Tracy and his followers reject metaphysical presuppositions as the doctrine of transcendent data, his *Elements of Ideology* is tacitly based on the metaphysical presupposition that nature is a well-ordered cosmos in which everything happens in accordance with knowable laws or ideas. The first meaning of the term "ideology" as the system of ideas governing society finds its origin here.

Napoleon I is responsible for the rise of the second meaning of the term.[2] The "ideologists" of the Enlightenment were not directly involved in the practical politics of that time because of the effective separation between morality and politics. Nevertheless, their moral views did not fail to exercise an indirect influence on political events. At first, Napoleon was on friendly terms with the "ideologists" and for some time even he himself became a member of their institute. But after 1803 a break occurred. Following the Enlightenment, the ideologists believed in the value of individual freedom, and this led to a conflict with the practical politics of Napoleon, whose regime increasingly strangled freedom. As freethinkers, moreover, the ideologists believed in the power of reason and could not reconcile themselves with Napoleon's tactical use of religion as an instrument of politics. The dictator Napoleon, who wanted a "realistic" policy, then called the views of the ideologists "ideological," in the sense of being ignorant of the world and adhering to vague metaphysics. Even in contemporary usage, the term "ideology" still continues to retain this meaning. Moreover, positivism and empiricism have reinforced this negative overtone.

The third meaning of "ideology" as pseudo-reasoning and alienation comes mainly from Marx and Engels. For Marx, ideas are images and mirror reflections of the infrastucture, they echo the situation existing in the realm of production. On the other hand, he ascribes to these ideas and images a critical function with respect to the infrastructure. Thus, the ideas which arise from the infrastructure can affirm or modify the infrastructure by a kind of feedback. This Marxist view of ideas vacillates between vulgar materialism and speculative idealism. According to Marx, there are real conceptions and true ideas—those that agree with the infrastructure—but there are also illusory conceptions and false ideas—those that are out of harmony with the forces and the relationships of production. Thus a distinction must be made between ideology and ideas. For Marx, ideologies are mainly illusory conceptions or false ideas. In his earliest works, however, he sometimes uses the term "ideology" also in a positive sense; for instance, he speaks there about his own view as a scientific ideology.

In Marx's doctrine ideas pass through three phases. In the first phase they exercise a preparatory function and assist in letting the changing infrastructure break through in the superstructure. For instance, the bourgeois ideas have done their share in overthrowing feudal society. The second phase is that of victory. The new mode of production, which embraces both the forces of production and the relationships of production, is affirmed and confirmed by the ideas of the suprastructure. It is the period of temporary harmony. This period is followed by the ideological phase in the proper sense, the period of decline. With high-sounding phrases the ruling class tries to camouflage the wretched condition of the social system and to counteract the new evolution of the forces and relationships of production.[3]

The essence of the ideological consciousness, then, lies here in the inability to know the historical-social situation. A split occurs between the world of the material infrasturcture and that of the ideological superstructure, represented by theology, philosophy, ethics, etc. The source of this split, says Marx, lies in both the division of labor and the alienation of labor. First of all, the division of labor caused a split between material and spiritual work, between manual labor and intellectual work. Those who perform intellectual work create an object of their own and, like Hegel, they plunge into a world of spiritual entities, which they view as the driving forces of society and history. The second cause of the ideological alienation lies in the estrangement of labor. One of the results of the division of labor is that man becomes alienated from the product of his work. This product—capital—becomes a power in itself, imposes itself on man's consciousness and leads to alienating ideas.

These considerations can be briefly summarized as follows. The ideology has its origin, on the one hand, in the ideas of the superstructure which is built on the alienation of the economic infrastructure, and on the other hand, in the economic alienation of the superstructure which, by separating itself from manual labor, leads a life of its own.[4]

The preceding paragraphs show how the three variant definitions of ideology arose in history. But before we can proceed to a critical comparison of utopia and ideology, we must still pursue the historical development of the ideology after Marx.

In the second half of the nineteenth century the rationalism of the Enlightenment began to weaken and belief in a natural order, a natural equilibrium and a naturally continuous progress disappeared. This gave rise to all kinds of irrational trends. Men like Schopenhauer, Nietzsche, Sorel and Pareto distrusted the power of man's insight into truth and pleaded for irrationality. The evolution of science and technology disturbed the harmonious order of nature and this played havoc with the rationalistic ideas of the Enlightenment. Schopenhauer countered the optimism of the Enlightenment, with its faith in the continuity of progress, with the pessimistic remark that our world is the worst possible. In his eyes it is not reason and idea which drive man, but will. For Nietzsche truth is something which interests only men of learning. Truth is a way of erring without which, it must be granted, man cannot live, but the proper driving forces of life are the passions. Pareto views truth only in function of power which tries to maintain its position. In his eyes arguments are "derivations," which merely serve to camouflage the "residue," the sum total of unconscious intentions which influence one's actions. Sorel is of the opinion that the objective insight into truth, if it is possible at all, kills man's impetus. Man needs myths, ideologies and illusions to get into action. Man's irrational need for ideology must be fostered.

In this irrational trend the ideology assumes the form of the social myth spoken of in the preceding chapter. It becomes a dog-matized conviction of having a mission. Rejecting any possible cri-tique of ideology by denying every criterion of truth, this theory of total ideology evaporates into thin air. When no cognitive value is ascribed to ideas in either true or false forms but attention is paid only to immediate power relationships, then the use of the term "ideology" is virtually meaningless. The social myth then takes over the place of the ideology and represents its total control over the masses as control by these masses themselves.

In the 1920s a new element entered into the history of the prob-lem of ideology. After the preparatory work of Dilthey, Scheler and Weber, it was especially Mannheim who, in his "sociology of knowl-edge," made room for the theory of ideology in modern sociology. In the "sociology of knowledge" the ideology is approached from a new angle. According to Mannheim, the theory of ideology has as its task to unmask the more or less deliberate lies and smokescreens behind which groups and especially political parties hide, but the sociology of knowledge investigates how social standpoints are of necessity conditioned by the social context. His sociology of knowl-edge wishes to develop a systematic study of the different social standpoints. In the language of Francis Bacon, it is a broad socio-logical "theory of idols." According to his sociology of knowledge, a critique of ideology is not possible because the entire structure of our thinking is determined by the historical totality of a particu-lar societal context.[5]

Mannheim makes a distinction here between particular ideology and radical or total ideology. The ideology is particular if it is con-cerned with certain statements and ideas of a subject which arise from his own psychological prejudices. With respect to such a particular ideology it is still possible, Mannheim thinks, to con-vince an opponent that his standpoint is prejudiced or distorted. But in the case of a total ideology one deals with a subject as repre-senting a particular class, culture or era, in other words, he repre-sents a collective subject. No critique of ideology is possible here because the societal context wholly determines the structure of con-sciousness.[6]

Mannheim's view that critique of ideas is not possible with respect to the over-all standpoint of society, but only with respect to a particular psychological level, actually formalizes the concept of ideology. The problem as to which ideas are true and which false is given up in favor of a mere formalization of social standpoints. The spirit of positivism triumphs here and ideas are relegated to the realm of subjective fancy and arbitrariness.[7]

Mannheim, however, is not entirely happy with the pan-ideologism to which his ideas seem to lead. That's why he makes a distinction between philosophical relativism and sociological relationism, and argues that his theory must be viewed as relationism. By this he means that knowledge doesn't capitulate before historical relativity and situationalism. He rejects philosophical relativism, understood as purely historical arbitrariness without any norms. But he acknowledges that our knowing always comes about, and has to come about, within the context of a certain concrete society and is, therefore, to that extent, relational. Ideologizing influences, he holds, cannot be eliminated, but they can be mitigated by a systematic analysis of the largest possible number of varying standpoints. The different social groups, Mannheim adds, are unequal in their ability to transcend their own standpoint, but the best expectations can be placed on the groups of intellectuals, at least if they are not directly tied to a particular class.

Mannheim's "relationism" shows that he doesn't wish to give up entirely the idea of criticizing ideology, but he lacks any demonstrable norm to determine what the right consciousness is. His sociology of knowledge can only offer formal assistance; that's why it is vehemently opposed especially by such neo-Marxist writers as Max Horkheimer, Theodor Adorno and Jürgen Habermas of the "School of Frankfurt."

In our time three different positions are taken with respect to values and ideas as normative of social life. In these three trends the term "ideology" has, as we will see, sometimes a positive meaning but also, on other occasions, a purely negative sense.

The first trend is formed by a number of prominent sociologists, who defend the thesis that the ideological era is coming to an end.

Among these we may name Aron,[8] Bell,[9] Brunner[10] and Schelsky.[11] These sociologists not only oppose the ideology but also think that in the post-bourgeois industrial society there really isn't any room left for social ideas. They hate ideologies because of their experiences with all kinds of leftist and rightist totalitarian systems around World War II, which appealed to such political ideas. But they also hold that in the bourgeois societies of the past ideologies were the inevitable substitutes for the disappearing religious and metaphysical views of man and the world. Since the social sciences had not yet sufficiently come of age, one had to have recourse to semi-scientific ideas. According to these sociologists, it is to be expected that in the industrial society the socio-political decisions will in the long run be made in a totally rational way, that is to say, they will be inspired by scientific considerations. Habermas calls this view the technocratic model according to which both the means and the goals will be set by the sciences.[12]

Schelsky thinks that in fact, as a result of scientific-technological development, the role of the ideology will be increasingly replaced by "the law-abidance which governs an apparatus" and by "the internal necessity of things." Bell concedes that "the end of ideology is not—and should not be—the end of utopia as well,"[13] but his concept of utopia has shrivelled down to an empirical-scientific prognosis and planning of the future in terms of the present. The very expectation, however, that the empirical sciences will in the long run skillfully express what hitherto has been done unskillfully by an ideology, is itself something ideological. This positivistic rationalism is just as irrational and dogmatic as the ideological concept which it combats.

The second, and until recently the most popular, trend thinks that man's actions are ultimately based on a non-rational option with respect to values and purposes. It assumes the standpoint of relativism with regard to values. The only ethic which still remains standing above this relativistic standpoint for which all values and ideas are equally valid, is the idea that in a pluralistic society one must accept a plurality of views about life with tolerance. Habermas speaks in this connection of the decisionistic model, which goes back to Weber's sociological positivism. Weber is known as the great protagonist of a value-free science. He wants to solve the problem of value and truth, of "ought" and "is," of faith and reason by way of compromise. The realm of ideas and of worldviews is autonomous, as is that of science. In this decisionistic model values are irrationally determined by faith or philosophy, so that it is the task of science to find rationally the means for bringing these irrational ideas to realization.

In this second trend of thought the term "ideology" has sometimes a positive and something a negative meaning. Some writers ascribe a positive sense to the term and reserve it for the realm of ideas and values in contrast to the autonomous realm of science. Others conceive the ideology in a negative way and call ideological those views of life which dogmatically attack the autonomy of value-free science. All these writers, however, defend the thesis that science is value-free and wish to keep its realm free either from ideas or from ideologies. But this positivism, which investigates only "reality as it is," is itself based on an evaluating attitude of mind because its scientific research is marked by the contemporary values of the *status quo*. The thesis that science is value-free is, as a matter of fact, based on an assumed "ideology of objectivity."

The technocratic model, we saw, wishes to reduce the ideas to the realm of scientific investigation, and the decisionistic trend views ideas as a matter of faith which is foreign to the rationalism of science. A third trend tries to connect science and values. Wright, Adorno, Horkheimer and Habermas argue that, on the one hand, the ideas must constantly be checked against the results of scientific inquiry and that, on the other, the sciences must keep referring to the interpretative frameworks of the ideas. Especially the neo-Marxist "School of Frankfurt" has done trailblazing work in this matter. Adorno, Horkheimer[14] and Habermas[15] with their critical theory plead that the sciences must be viewed critically in the light of an over-all vision of man and society. This point constitutes the critical core of the theory. Reversely, the historical totality in its development must be analyzed scientifically. This constitutes the scientific core of the critique.

Habermas calls this the pragmatistic model, according to which there exists a dialectical relationship between ideas and the sciences. The critical theory emphasizes the value of critical ideas as a source of inspiration for man's scientific inquiry. This theory wants to unmask the ideologies, which it views in the negative sense of pretexts, self-deceptions and blind faith. The pragmatistic model claims that the positivistic criteria of empirical verifiability advocated by the technocratic model are, just like the ideals of irrational mystical certainty advocated by the decisionistic model, expressions of two distinct but closely connected ideological attitudes.

The representatives of the "School of Frankfurt" also point to the typical form assumed by contemporary ideology. There exists, they think, a close connection between positivism's ideology of objectivity and the consumer civilization. Both phenomena, they claim, arise from the compulsion to conform to the existing situation, that is to say, to follow the existing patterns of consumption imposed by the system. That's why the ideology dominating in the consumer society differs in an important respect from the classical concept of ideology. The classical ideology possesses a camouflaging function. High-sounding words and pseudo-arguments are used by private interests to cover up the existing situation. Wrong as it is, this justification shows that man does not wish to dwell on the level of crude reality but experiences a need to view his actual desires and wants as "ideal." Positivism's technocratic consciousness, for which science is a fetish, is, on the one hand, less ideological than were the former ideologies because it takes a critical attitude with respect to irrational values, but on the other hand, it is also much more ideological because it suppresses the need for moral justification. According to Habermas, the classical ideologies are "only ideologies," they are born from the desire for justification[16] but the positivistic ideology is a total ideology because it eliminates even the desire for justification.

The very possibility of transcendence and critique is taken away here. The ideological illusion is thus more concealed and more difficult to detect. The modern ideology is not only a false consciousness but also the oppression of a false consciousness. Marcuse calls the existing mass civilization one-dimensional, in opposition to the former bourgeois civilization in which there was still a measure of pluri-dimensionality. Formerly one could still practice a kind of humanity in the family circle, so that the possibility of criticizing continued to exist.[17] But the consumer civilization suppresses even this possibility. The opiate of consumption makes man be satisfied with the situation as it is and it dopes him in such a way that he cannot even be different from what he is. Consumption and positivism by their reciprocal action make reality one-dimensional. People, says Adorno, "in a faith without faith cling to pure existence,"[18] while they ought to live in the tension between what is and what can be, between existence and essence, between theory and praxis.

After this lengthly explanation of the contemporary positions with respect to ideas and ideologies, it is time to raise the question about the relationship between utopia and ideology. We will first present the views of Mannheim and Bloch, who have explicitly dealt with this problem, and then present our own opinion.

Mannheim places both utopias and ideologies under the same common label of representation which "transcends being."[19] These transcendent representations are, according to him, strangers to reality—the opposite of representations which "agree with being." By "being" or reality he means the concrete historical form of society. The criterion to distinguish between ideological and utopian representations which "transcend being" lies on the level of reality. Ideological representations, Mannheim holds, "conceal reality" and thus are in fact never realized. The ruling conservative classes love to resort to transcendent ideas to camouflage reality. But to the utopian representation Mannheim ascribes a force capable of "transforming reality." These utopian ideas possess a trailblazing function and they exist especially among oppressed classes which try to become emancipated.

The crucial point in Mannheim's view is how and when one can determine whether conceptions foreign to reality are ideological or utopian. The only answer is that subsequent evidence will show whether the conception was an ideology or a utopia, depending on whether is was not or was transformed into reality. But with respect to a present conception is it difficult to arrive at a conclusion.

In actual fact, all this means that Mannheim adheres to a positivistic standpoint. He detaches that which *de facto* is from its possibilities of future developments. He limits himself to the empirical situation of facts and does not see that the real situation presents real possibilities and tendencies for the future, both on the part of the object and on that of the subject. The dualism of Weber's decisionistic model with its separate realms of irrationality and rationality recurs here under the new names of "foreign to being" and "congruent with being." The utopia is here in itself foreign to reality and irrational although it can subsequently turn out to be congruent with being and rational. With his scientistic attitude Mannheim does not see that two kinds of rationality and reality must be distinguished but not separated, viz., on the one hand, scientific rationality and empirical reality in the narrow sense, and on the other, hermeneutic rationality and the reality of life in the broad sense. This "enlarged reason" or "context-dependent rationality," as the recognition and understanding of certain collective values, precisely offers the interpretative framework within which alone facts can appear and receive their character of reality.[20]

Mannheim doesn't recognize the figure-horizon relationship between functional reason and enlarged reason; that's why he fails to notice the essential dialectics of the utopia as far horizon. The utopia is for him sheer distance without horizon at one moment—namely, when its representation is still "alien to reality." But at another moment, the one at which its representation has been brought about in reality, has become "congruent with being," the utopia is a horizon without distance. If Mannheim took the trailblazing function of the utopia, its "power to transform reality" seriously, he should stop calling the utopia "unreal." But, as a matter of fact, he conceives the utopia as a kind of ideology—namely, a rationalization that is foreign to reality but, nonetheless, subsequently turns out to play a role.[21]

Bloch, we saw, is the second writer who has extensively dealt with the problem of the utopia and particularly its relationship to ideology. He began writing about it in his book *The Spirit of Utopia* (1918) and since then he has continued thinking about it. After the collapse of the German Nazi "reality," he published his work *Freedom and Order* (1946). He there shows how only through the "process-like concrete" utopia freedom and order attain "objective mediation" and thus lose their irreconcilable polarization as opposites. And in his three volume work *The Principle of Hope* (1949) Bloch explains how the utopia is the real anticipation of the new dimension in human history.

Bloch wishes to strip the utopia of its pejorative meaning as the fanciful dreams of people who want to improve the world but are strangers to its reality. For this reason he introduces the distinction between concrete and abstract utopias. Abstract utopias are sheer fancies, whose anticipations of the future are in no way connected with history and the present. Such abstract utopias evaporate into "sheer utopizing" and end up with an "empty possibility." Concrete utopias, on the other hand, aim at a realistically possible goal and also indicate concrete ways of reaching it. They anticipate the "really possible." These anticipations of the utopian *novum* make an appeal to both the heart and the intellect.[22]

Bloch then tries to explain the ideology in terms of the utopia and makes a distinction in the concept of ideology. In the spirit of Marx he first ascribes a camouflaging function to the ideology. It is the product of a "false consciousness," a complex of ideas to which truth is ascribed, not because of its inner power of conviction, but because of the class interest which is justified and protected by these ideas.

But, Bloch adds, many ideologies have also a different dimension. There are ideological ideas which are purely ideological, but there are also others which, as ideas, fulfill a utopian function. These ideologies, because of their utopian dimension, continue to have a meaningful significance even for other times. Bloch is referring here to the masterpieces of civilization in the realms of art, science, religion and philosophy. These works of the superstructure utopically also have something to say to the new era, even though their ideological significance has vanished after the collapse of the social infrastructure. Such works of art as the Acropolis of the Greeks' slave-holding society and the many cathedrals of feudal serfdom should not be complained about, although they arose on a foundation that is now superseded and which was unworthy of man.[23]

Bloch thinks that the utopian function is the "principle of hope" for a human race which assumes responsibility for its own destiny. Through the utopia the history of mankind becomes a meaningful and hopeful task because it doesn't grow old in what is already established but rejuvenates itself in what is new, without jumping into the blind adventure of abstract utopias.

We have now reached the stage where an attempt can be made to circumscribe the question of the relationship between utopia and ideology in a definitive way. It is Bloch, I think, who has most correctly approached this problem. But we will return later to the question whether Bloch's "principle of hope," with its intraworldly utopian horizon, does not receive an even broader and deeper expectation through Christian eschatological hope.

The contemporary call for continuing education and unceasing critique of society means, I think, that we are getting closer to the end of the ideological era. The makers of the technocratic model had some inkling of this truth, but drew the wrong conclusion that science should be value-free. They rightly opposed the bourgeois ideologies of the eighteenth and nineteenth centuries, which in our eyes are too dogmatic and irrational. Our modern time which, following the evolution of science and technology, knows that it is responsible for the future, itself must give meaning to the future. The political ideologies of the past century are in decline. One can refer here to the conservative ideology of absolute rulers and higher classes, which ruled by "the grace of God," to the liberal ideology which was based on the natural order of individual interests in the capitalistic economy, and of the orthodox Marxist ideology, which dogmatically explains Marx's doctrine in the direction of a deterministic dialectical development.[24] Because of their *a priori* views these ideologies appear uncritical to us today. The technocratic model rightly opposes them, but falls into the opposite extreme of the ideology of objectivity. If it had substituted a critical value orientation in the sciences for the ideological orientation, as was done by the pragmatistic model, it would have avoided that extreme.

Ideology appears to be an antiquated concept, connected with the dualistic view of reality which has dominated our civilization since the Renaissance. When Western thought got rid of metaphysical and religious *a priori* views, it lapsed into a new dualism—the dualism of subject and object, of idealism and empiricism, of internal ethical action and external political action, of private freedom and social order. The ideology kept trying to overcome this dualism and this polarization between subject and empirical facticity by weakening one of these poles and placing in within the other pole's sphere of influence. The result was a mixture of faith and science. As Bloch rightly remarks, the two poles of freedom and order can only reach a higher integration within the totality of a dialectical process in which they retain their distinction.

The political ideas of the eighteenth and nineteenth centuries, such as Marx's scientific socialism and the "natural order" of liberalism, pretend to be based on a purely scientific foundation, but in actual fact they are camouflaged beliefs. This gives to the ideology its typical ambivalence as a dogmatic faith in the guise of science and as a science in the guise of a faith. The dogmatic religious horizon of the Middle Ages was simply replaced by a dogmatic secularized horizon in these ideologies. The ideological worldview took the place of the religious worldview, but retained the same need for dogmatic security. Even when people continue to hold fast to a religious belief in a world byond the grave, the need for an ideological anchorage makes itself felt. For example, for some time now the Catholic Church has had a Catholic social doctrine, which is an ideological mixture of religious *a priori* positions and empirical certainties.

The classical ideology tries to resolve the separation and the dualism of values and facts by pressuring the facts into the straitjacket of ideologies. The ideology brings the external world which is estranged from the subject again within the subject's reach. In the technocratic ideologies of positivism, however, the polarization occurs in the opposite direction. The subject is estranged there from the external world, and the ideology of objectivity tries to bring this subject to an acceptance of the existing world.

The dualism and opposite polarization of subjectivism and empiricism, of transcendence and facticity are solved by the classical ideologies of the bourgeois era and by the positivistic ideology of the post-bourgeois period in the one-sided direction of either an ideal transcendence or an empirical facticity. Only a dialectical process is able to make the poles of transcendence and facticity merge in a "mediated" unity in which both retain their relative autonomy.

Following Husserl, A. C. van Peursen aptly calls this dialectical process "transcendental facticity,"[25] that is to say, facticity as both referring to the horizon and disclosing it. In this way he rejects, on the one hand, the transcendentism of those religious or philosophical attitudes which seek support in a transcendent reality independently of the empirical world. Such attitudes claim to know the supra-sensible more or less independently of the sensible. But "transcendental facticity" admits a transcendental dimension or horizon which discloses itself in the perceptible world as a "present absence."

The classical ideologies appear less capable for disclosing this horizon. They are too dogmatic and view the horizon of the future as an existing presence. They say too little about the future as *far* horizon and too much about it as far *horizon*. The ideology is too little vision and too much a system of ideas, it changes an open horizon into a closed horizon. Although the ideology has a trail-blazing function because of its horizon of the future, its closed character easily makes it exercise a camouflaging function. The ideological man lives in the illusion that he already knows the future as possibility and knows it exactly. One who thus takes his ideological principles as a clear starting point for evaluating the worldly situation, does, as a matter of fact, base himself on a standpoint that derives from an existing or even a past historical situation. That's why the classical ideologies of the bourgeois era are such a typical mixture of the past and the future, or petrifaction and renewal. The utopia, on the other hand, discloses the horizon not as a pure presence but as an absent presence. The main difference is that the ideological man acts *on the basis of* an ideological system while the utopian man acts *in the light of* a utopian portrayal.

The pure experience of reality as transcendental facticity also rejects positivism's ideology of objectivism, which claims to find its certainty in pure facts. Facticity as figure refers to a transcending horizon of meaning. Reality is "tendentious" in the good sense of the term. A so-called neutral or valuefree science says too little about facticity as "thrown *project*" and too much about it as "*thrown* project." A science which respects values rightly wishes to take the aspect of project, of "tendentious" directedness, into consideration because there exists a reciprocal relationship between fact and possibility.

Because of the tempestuous development of the sciences, modern society demands a dynamic source for the giving of meaning. The utopia must not only be heard from when the existing ideologies run aground. A dynamic evolution must constantly be guided by a sparkling vision of the future. Our time demands "permanent" or "continuing" education because contemporary man must learn to live with change. He can no longer rely on the dogmatic anchorage of ideologies. On the other hand, he must not drift rudderless, without any vision of the future, on the sea of changes. Through the utopia society creates for itself a horizon which doesn't have the closed character of the ideology. The utopian man keeps the horizon open without getting lost thereby in the infinitely distant. The picture of the future inspired by the utopian imagination is not presented as something directy known in itself, as the ideology unjustly claims, but only as mediately known through the negation of the present. The utopia offers a vision of the future in the light of which society can venture to go forward in an experimental fashion; it doesn't offer an ideology of the future in which the roads are clearly outlined. As Bloch succinctly expresses it, the utopia is nothing but "something that is kept open for a reality which is possible in the future but has not yet been decided upon and which could be brought about in that empty space."[26] Utopian thinking must constantly be *corrected* on the basis of experience, but, unlike ideological thought, it need not be *refuted*.[27]

The way contemporary man experiences reality demands the interplay of the concrete utopia and a science that doesn't shrink from "involvement." All this is accurately rendered by the term "transcendental facticity," which indicates that everything given has a referential and disclosing character. Facticity as referring to the horizon belongs to the realm of science, and facticity as disclosing the horizon is the task of critical vision or the concrete utopia. Undoubtedly one is entitled to replace the expression "critical vision" or "concrete utopia" by "critical" or "utopian ideology." A name is always more or less arbitrary. But I'd prefer to drop the word "ideology" because of its antiquated bourgeois connotation. The word "ideology" retains too much the unpalatable connotation of conservativism and rigidity, it lacks the utopian atmosphere of flexibility and playfulness.

10. THE EXPLORATORY VALUE OF THE UTOPIA

People suffering from a one-sided need for exactness attach to the term "utopian" the pejorative sense of fanciful dreaming. But without the utopian dimension man would not be fully a "being of possibilities" and a choice between alternatives. The essence of the utopia lies in what Ruyer calls "the utopian mode,"[1] that is to say, the utopia is the liberating impetus to keep transcending the limitations of human existence toward a better future. The utopia increases the resilience of the mind and inspires man's freedom to change and renewal.[2] The utopia is imagination in action in the realm of human pursuits. It tries to portray the possible future. But how can man know that which is not yet, that which is merely something that could be? The "rational intellect" which bases itself on the perception of facts cannot know such a new thing. It is the imagination which comes to the rescue of the analyzing intellect here. Without the imagination there exists only a world of facts and situations.[3] But through his fantasy man can reach behind and beyond the here and now, he can locate himself imaginatively elsewhere, in different conditions, in situations that are not yet present, in the future. The imagination can portray and express the possible. Man is distinguished from animals precisely by his ability to form such pictures.

The fact that in our time so little value is attached to creative imagination and that there is such a one-sided trust in the ideology of exactness indicates that we are strongly dominated by the existing situation, the *status quo*. For too long a time the asceticism of science has undervalued the power of imagination. Fantasy is precisely the unique power to imagine a future which is not yet actually present. The imaginary is largely independent of the actual and it makes human freedom an open-ended freedom. That's why the imagination is preferably associated with the ideas of unfulfillment, absence, openness, unlimited space, pure and free movement. Without the imagination man would not be a "movement of transcendence," he would remain glued to the past and the present without any elbowroom.

All this should not be taken to mean that scientific exactness must be surrendered to an uncontrolled play of fantasy. Science and utopian fantasy should complement each other. Science without utopian imagination clings to the present and leads to petrifaction. Such a science can only extrapolate the present and calculate the future in terms of this present. Its portrayal of the future is retrospective because it merely extends the lines of the present into the future. The utopia without scientific sense, on the other hand, runs wild and degenerates into pure fancy, it produces all kinds of "utopias of escape."[4] In such fancies the utopian man doesn't know what to do with reality and tries to escape from it by means of the ideal conditions of his dreams. It is only when science and utopia collaborate that man approaches the future in a prospective way. He then is in a rational manner open to new things in his exploration of the future.

The utopian approach is fundamentally different from the "planning" approach because it does not demand that its ideas be immediately realizable. The utopia is more a matter of presenting possibilities than of trying to bring them about. That's why the utopia is not an ideological program or system of guidelines to transform the world. The utopia presents possibilities and asks science to test the feasibility of their realization. It sketches a picture of the future which science must develop and refine. The utopia itself remains a playful thinking that reality could be different. Fantasy playfully distantiates itself from the existing *status quo* in order to view this status as relative and subject to change in the light of what appears possible to imaginative thinking. Because the utopia resolves the constituted world into a "cloud of possibilities," it functions as a pacemaker of revolutionary social changes.

The utopia enjoys more leeway than do the sciences. The imagination also plays an important role in scientific research, for instance, in the formulation of hypotheses. But its role there differs from that in the utopia. Although science is inventive, it tries to achieve the possible by strongly relying on the actual facts. But the utopian imagination likes to experiment with the entire complex of actual facts and its forte is to foresee the possibility of a different complex of facts.

Unlike scientific thinking, utopian thought need not at once to be verified or rejected. It can be brought to bloom or given more concrete contours only mediately, that is, by means of scientific thought. The realistic approach of science may not stray too far from the realm of hard facts. But for the idealistic utopia the realm of facts is only the starting point from which it can rise to the horizon of unlimited possibilities. The utopian element corresponds to the creative nature of man, who is possibility rather than facticity. Utopian thought expands the sum total of possibilities expected by science by adding to it a number of unexpected possibilities. Utopian fantasy breaks with the familiar and rationalized combinations, it breaks through the repressive crust of the constituted and brings to consciousness things which have not yet come to be. Kolakowski calls the utopia the necessary condition of every revolutionary change "because there is . . . an experience which teaches us that goals that cannot now be realized can never be realized unless one sets them at a moment when they cannot yet be realized. In other words, what at a given moment is impossible becomes only possible at a different moment if it was held to be possible when it was still impossible."[5] The utopian mind believes in the possibility that everything always remains subject to renovation.

The utopian man is playful, and this is why utopian portrayals have a playful and liberating character. Fantasy thoughtfully plays with reality and playfully thinks of it. That's why the imagination is said to "play" and not to "work." Like a play, the utopian fantasy moves between two extremes. The lower limit is the realm of reality, in the sense of facticity, the upper limit is the realm of the unreal, of unbridled fancy. One can best compare this situation to playing.[6] As is well-known, people beset with anxiety do not dare to play. They are afraid of the imagination and camouflage this with the rationalization that they want to remain as close as possible to the facts. But the everyday world of what is already is not the only avenue of escape for the anxious man, as is clearly illustrated by the child. He can also take refuge in the fantasy world of play. Because the anxious man is unable to cope with the conflicts of life, he builds a fictitious world alongside the real world. This fictitious world remains a defense against these conflicts because it is the place where unfulfilled and repressed desires find their compensation.

The utopian attitude moves in between these two extreme boundaries in a similar fashion. A society which clings too much to facticity, to the existing order, loses its freedom as creative power in the constituted world and lives under the violence of petrifaction. The inert field offers no leeway for change and renewal. Such a self-estranged one-dimensional society can have but little appreciation of utopian thinking. In its eyes the utopia is a childish and foolish pastime. Such a society is in danger of becoming wholly petrified. In classical language, it gets stranded on the rocks of Scylla.

It can also happen, however, that the utopia itself becomes a realm of alienation. Even as man in his playing can let his imagination run away with him to such an extent that he can no longer distinguish between play and reality, so also is there a danger that utopian fantasy becomes an escape from reality. Unable to cope with the conflicts of reality, the imagination can run wild. Stripped of any healthy sense of reality, it indulges in nebulous speculations. These "utopias of escape" become a danger and assume a totalitarian form when they are mistaken for pictures of a real world. The utopia then loses its playful character and its openness. It no longer plays with the possibility that things could be different but degenerates into an authoritarian wishful dreaming of social myths or, if it is less powerful, into a dogmatic hammering on ideological positions.

The history of utopian thought offers numerous examples of such degenerations. They are products of fanciful dreamers who are trying to escape from themselves and seek salvation in a world of fancy. They wish to make their dreamt "salvation" a "real" world. History shows how the immediate—and consequently dogmatic—introduction of utopias always results in failure and disaster. We may refer here to the Platonic experiment of the perfect State, the experiments of the utopian socialists Saint-Simon, Fourier and Proudhon, and the totalitarian doctrine of salvation embodied in the Third Reich. A society which ventures into trying such fancies perishes in chaos; in classical language, it cannot avoid the maelstrom of Charybdis.

A healthy utopia offers a new perspective on man and society, but its content must be given further shape by means of experience inspired by the utopia. Utopia and "topography" must go hand in hand, i.e., the utopia is the portrayal of a social ideal which is not dogmatically fixed but varies according to the historical time and culture. This portrayal of the ideal functions as a guideline for social thinking and acting, and it makes us more aware of the imperfections of the existing social reality.

For a good understanding of the character proper to utopian thinking one must keep in mind the ambiguity of human freedom. Man's freedom stands between possibility and facticity, portrayal and actual reality, project and thrownness. Man is the only being in which the potential holds primacy over facticity, but even this potential is a real possibility only on the basis of his facticity.

This is why the utopia has too little power of imagination if it is only a picture of facticity. On the other hand, it has too much power of imagination if it deduces reality itself from its portrayal. This means that the utopia can become self-estranged in the world as well as alienated from the world. The right equilibrium arises when there is a dialectical relationship between utopia and reality (or science). Science without utopia becomes too fossilized, utopia without science becomes sheer fancy. But a playful concrete utopia enlarges the field of vision and opens many new perspectives. On the one hand, it guards men's thinking against escaping into empty speculations because of its empirical starting point; on the other it prevents the inertia of settling down in what is already the case because of its imaginative distantiation from the existing situation.

11. The Normative Value of the Utopia

The utopia corresponds to the nature of man, who is possibility rather than facticity. The utopian mood wishes to foster the feeling that things could be different. Its vision of the future is explorative but, at the same time, also ethically normative. There are writers who want to strip the utopia of its normative ethical character and conceive the utopia as a purely instrumental and explorative category. For example, W. Mündel pays one-sidedly too much attention to the explorative function and not enough to the normative aspect of the contemporary utopia when he describes it as the transition from the "ideal state" to the "neutral instrument."[1] Such a view is a complete denial of the utopian intention, which is precisely directed to the liberation of man and the humanization of the world, the "perspective on the prospective."[2] In addition to, or rather precisely in, its inventiveness, the utopia also has a critical normative function. It wishes to put the present in the light of a new future more worthy of man. The other possible world functions as a "mirror of conscience," in which the actual situation is reflected as less free and falling short of what man ought to be.

It is the nature of man to be critical, that is to say, he evaluates his situation in the light of an ideal or norm; this is why the utopian approach is in keeping with man's inmost character. Critique lies at the source of all human progress. In the light of imaginary pictures of the future, man experiences his own situation as imperfect and notices the prevailing evil conditions. By placing oneself on a normative standpoint, one distantiates oneself from the actual situation and views the existing achievements as relative. The ethical man is the free man who can say "no" with respect to the ties binding him to the existing situation and thus transcend it. He holds that "what is can not be true."

There is something strange about the norm which doesn't express what is but what ought to be. Man has only a vague knowledge of this norm. By positing norms, one enters, as it were, into the void of non-being. The norm is the "void in which possible changes"[3] can occur. The precise content of the norms is "nowhere," but man as possibility is the being which in this "nowhere" tries to find the meaning and direction of the limited and actual "somewhere" with which he deals in daily life.[4] The paradoxical relationship between the actual and the norm, between what I encounter in my situation and what is a hidden possibility of the future, may be clarified by the figure-horizon relationship. The figure is what I perceive immediately, it is present. The world in its future possibilities is the background, it is still absent. Because no background can appear without a figure and no figure without a background, the figure discloses the background as a "present absence." Man has an implicit idea of the horizon of meaning by the fact that he explicitly knows that the figure is limited; conversely, he knows explicitly that the figure is limited because he has implicit knowledge of the horizon of meaning. A simple example can serve to illustrate what has been said here about the knowledge of norms. When I sit down in a chair and say that it is not comfortable, I can make this explicit statement becaue I implicitly realize that a more comfortable chair is possible, even if I do not yet have an explicit and clearly defined conception of such a chair. The chair is evaluated as uncomfortable against the background idea of a better chair; at the same time, I only become aware of this better chair in the background because this chair here in the foreground does not please me at all.

Critical negativity, then, is an essential aspect of the utopia. Any vision of the future will always contain much critique of the existing situation. The utopia knows the stage of negation, in which it antithetically takes a position against the existing society. As one can see in the classical example of Thomas More, the writer begins with a penetrating analysis of the evils afflicting Europe and especially England at that time, and only then proceeds to paint a picture of the ideal society, his "ideal island" in the second part of his *Utopia*. More, however, obviously did not wish to transform the world according to the model he sketched of this island. The perfect State is also meant as a kind of raillery. It functions as a portrayal of the idea in which society can observe a playful picture of its imperfections and thus place itself at a distance from the actual conditions. More is the man who discovered the value of the utopian negation.

Society has a mainly negative knowledge of the horizon of the future which it seeks. The negative dialectics with respect to what has already been achieved offers an intuitive presentiment of the future. That's why writers such as Bloch, Marcuse, Adorno[5] and Kosik[6] rightly emphasize that man and society must view the existing situation antithetically, protestingly and dialectically if they wish to become aware of new real possibilities. The future of a better world toward which man is on the way discloses itself mainly in a negative way through the opposite experience of situations unworthy of man, such as oppression and exploitation. The logic of protest (Marcuse), the system of the antisystem (Adorno) constitute the critical negativity which keep alive man's consciousness that he is possibility rather than facticity.

The value of this negative "mediation" should not be underestimated. It is a positive force in establishing a united front against unfreedom and injustice. It enables society not to let the opiate of self-satisfaction put to sleep the desire for a better future and to fill the "appealing void" with the fetishes of "reifications." Every utopian model of the future is born from a critique on existing evil conditions, a dissatisfaction with the prevailing situation of society.

Many people who belong to the Establishment see in the youthful negativism an argument to disregard the call for a critical society. They underestimate the power emanating from critical negativity. The positive content of what is desired for society cannot always be immediately formulated. At first, one knows about this desire only in a negative way in the protesting attitude against the existing situation.

It is not right to qualify all forms of protest as nothing but dangerous negativism, but on the other hand, it is also wrong to value every protest as a critical distantiation from the present. Some protesters forget that critical negativity has value only as a *mediation* and ascribe to negativity a value in itself. One can protest for the sake of protest and demonstrate for the sake of demonstrating, as something that is exciting and attractive. In such a case narcissism, argumentative arrogance, aggressive frustration and intellectual snobbery exercise too much influence. As Duyvendak expresses it, training is needed even for learning how to say "no."[7] Protest may and must show a healthy aggressiveness, but it must not degenerate into the terrorism of agitators. Violent agitation doesn't make people become conscious of conflicts and doesn't lead to clarification of issues, but produces exactly the opposite effect. The agitator has become too much a victim of the existing frustrating situation; his "no" is not a mediating "no," it is not a liberating disavowal of that situation. His negation expresses itself in uncritical simplifications. One who merely limits himself to pointing out evil conditions without indicating concrete alternative roads, merely succeeds in making the situation go from bad to worse. T. Elbert warns against such an uncritical and irrational negation when he says: "Such people could easily one day become the prisoners of, on the one hand, mob-rule, and on the other, authoritarian repression."[8]

Sheer negation of, and distantiation from the actual situation is only what Merleau-Ponty calls the "hollow counterpart" of existing reality. Worse even, the sheer negation of, or opposition to the existing reality remains under the influence of this reality and functions in terms of it. It doesn't escape the domain of the constituted but remains in this domain as a negation. The Left which has no content of its own remains the Right. Although negation as distantiation from facticity codetermines creative freedom, it does this in relation with a positive perspective on the future. It is precisely in positing future possibilities that man finds the strength to transcend the existing state of affairs. Negative experiences with this existing state, however, make society conscious of the fact that something which should or could be is missing, and to this extent the negation has a mediating character. But the human mind can form a picture of the possible and thus is able to transcend the actual limitations. Although the negation in itself leads to distantiation, it doesn't lead to a transcendence of what actually is. It is precisely the idea of the possible which makes man come to a new project. As Adorno rightly says, "Society becomes a problem only to one who can conceive it as different from what it is."[9]

Especially among dialectical thinkers the negation is a matter of much controversy. In utopian dialectics, however, the antithesis always contains a positive aspect. Destructive critique of the present and a constructive vision of the future go hand in hand here. The negation always shows a glimmer of the true man and the true future. The authentic utopian mood does not refer to a transcendent realm, a transcendence beyond the existing human reality, but refers precisely to a transcendental dimension *of* this reality. This means that the progress of history must include a transcendence and that transcendence is possible only through the progress of history.

Several dialecticians speak only about progress without including any transcendence, while others strive too much for transcendence without progress. In either case the dialectical equilibrium is disturbed. The first group gets stuck in negation, and the second in transcending the negation. According to the French dialectician L. Goldmann, this situation is rather characteristic of the entire "School of Frankfurt." Its representatives make too sharp a distinction between the positive and the negative aspect of dialectics; thus they face the choice of either directing themselves negatively to the existing situation or assuming a positive utopian position outside this situation.[10]

According to these negative dialecticians, the only thing we can do is "nihilate" the situations; there is no positive image of the future toward which men can go forward together. The only thing positive is to say "no" to the situation, for the positivity of tomorrow is wholly and entirely hidden by today's negativity. Mankind is doomed to the prospectless process of gains and losses. Every forward step is converted into a backward step. Gain and loss are perfectly equal and neutralize each other. This is a new version of the ancient myth of Sisyphus.

There is some justification for the reproach addressed to Adorno that he advocates a prospectless going forward without any guideline. Goldmann criticizes Adorno's negativity, his "negative dialectics,"[11] which too exclusively insists on an exasperating continuation of dialectics. Kofler[12] also objects that Habermas indulges in a "contingent" dialectics. Although Habermas starts from the contrasts existing in reality and wishes to reduce them to a harmonious synthesis, he begins at a contingent and arbitrary point. He lacks the over-all vision by which one can discover the true negations and "sublate" them to a higher level. According to Aron, Sartre also condemns mankind to the cycle of alienation in the practico-inert field, followed by liberation through action and then again relapse into the estrangement of the practico-inert field.[13] In all these writers there is a "no" to the situation, a "no" that is constantly renewed and may never be given up, but which, nonetheless, does not succeed. The rebellion thus is in danger of being asphyxiated in its own negations. One goes forward but without any transcendent prospect. Many Marxist-Leninist dialecticians in particular are unable to recognize themselves in this new version of Marxism because Marx himself, they say, admitted a transcendent prospect. For Marx, they say, the transcendent subject is the oppressed class of proletarians, and this class has a prospect of the future.

The second group is too interested in transcendence without going forward by stages. Marcuse is a typical representative of this trend. Unlike writers of the first group, Marcuse knows the utopian prospect, but he is so interested in transcendence that he disregards the *topoi*, the intermediary stages one must pass through on the way to *utopia*, he wants to transcend without going forward through them. Because Marcuse's views have become rather popular, we will examine them a little more extensively.

Marcuse views his utopia—the negation of the negation—as that which is "wholly other" than the existing situation. The road to this "wholly other," the going forward to it, is thereby made practically impossible. His negation as "the great refusal" is a total rejection of the "existing society." The Marcusian "no" thus is too much an "unmediated" negation. This negation lives on the anarchistic idea that one can build society from the ground up by starting from a paradise-like point-zero. First the existing order must be abolished and then "the reign of freedom" can be constructed from absolute zero. Such a radical negation takes its position outside existing reality and thinks that society can be changed by a revolution from without. Lenin long ago warned against this kind of radicalism of the Left, calling it a childhood disease of communism. Although "the great refusal" has a lofty goal, it neglects to indicate how this goal is to be reached. Qualitative changes demand historical "mediations." It is just as impossible to leap directly from capitalism to socialism as from socialism to communism. Marcuse fails to indicate a road of intermediary goals by which the abyss between the present and the future can be bridged. Thus there is no possibility of really going forward.

While Habermas gets too involved in details because he lacks an overarching vision of the future, Marcuse with his thesis about the end of utopia wants to bring about the utopian horizon too immediately, without going forward on the mediating road of partial or steplike progress. Thus the open utopian horizon is in danger of becoming a closed ideology. There is then no break through one-dimensionality but merely a relocation of one-dimensionality from the level of existing reality to that of the ideal.

It is striking, again, that the most vehement criticism of Marcusian Marxism comes from the side of the Marxists themselves. According to Holz, himself a follower of Marxist thought, Marcuse doesn't do justice to the reality of the dialectics. He accuses him of ideologically separating theory and praxis. Not every form of opposition to the *status quo* qualifies as revolutionary. For example, at the beginning of the nineteenth century there existed a romantic opposition to the rising capitalism. This opposition produced a rebellious state of mind but was unable to bring about a revolutionary change of the social conditions. Marx and Engels themselves already combated such an opposition with their "critical critique" in *The Holy Family* and *The German Ideology*. They claimed that a theory whose truth can only lie in the praxis must start from the existing real possibilities. When a theory is too far removed from existing reality, it becomes an "empty theory" leading to a "blind praxis." As a dialectician, Holz accuses Marcuse of having forgotten the dialectical unity of theory and praxis. This disregard leads to ideology and a false consciousness. According to Holz, Marcuse's critical utopia is more like an intraworldly sectarian eschatology of salvation which knows only confessors and martyrs. The "wholly other" of this doctrine of salvation cannot be produced but only provoked.[14]

Moreover, thinks Holz, Marcuse makes a dialectical mistake with his unspecified abstract negation of "the great refusal." The dialectical negation is not a totally different, contradictory negation but a distinguishing, contrary negation. A contradictory negation excludes the thesis. It is *absolutely against* (*gegenstreitig*) it and precludes any development in the direction of a synthesis. A contrary opposition, on the other hand, aims at complementing the thesis. Contrary relationships are not "absolutely against," but merely compete with (*streitig*) each other, they are opposites moving in the direction of a synthesis.[15]

Dialectics is a process of growth in which existing reality is raised to a higher level of development by means of the contrary negation. The three moments of the dialectical process in their reciprocal tensions bring the development to a higher level. But in Marcuse these three moments are not merely distinguished but separated by the contradictory negation. What is must first be totally demolished by "the great refusal," and only then can the "wholly other" of the utopia be brought about.

According to Holz, Marcuse's undifferentiated use of repressive tolerance makes any strategy using intermediary goals impossible from the very start. The existing society also contains many more real possibilities that could be exploited. For example, if the existing society must allow man a semblance of freedom and satisfaction in order to make people insensitive to their oppression, it offers a primitive form of elbowroom. This means precisely that there are possibilities here in this semblance of freedom and satisfaction to make people aware of, and sensitive to authentic freedom and authentic needs.[16] Following Serge Mallet, Goldmann also thinks that a new working class of specialists, technicians and skilled workers is being formed. This class will become increasingly more conscious of the important role it plays in the process of production and will no longer be satisfied with the mere execution of work and decent wages. This class will raise the qualitative question, which is not; Do I get a raise? but: Do I have more to say? Can I get a greater share in the making of decisions?[17]

Holz accuses Marcuse of ideological abstractness—a mortal sin among Marxists with their insistence on concreteness and their aversion to ideology. The unspecified abstract refusal or negation dialectically results in an equally abstract and theoretical negation of the negation. The utopian portrayal of the future bears then the seal of vagueness and speculation, as is evident from such expressions as "the reign of freedom" or "pacified existence." The utopian "wholly other" is here, for lack of a concrete positive content, one-sidedly described as an abstract liberation from the present. In this fashion Marcuse's speculative theory is abstractly consistent.

Holz, the Marxist, fears that Marcuse's radicalism of the Left can easily block the road to the Marxist society. Either the Left impetus will quickly subside because the ideal lies beyond reach in abstract remoteness or, disenchanted, the impetus will assume an aggressive attitude of provocation, in which case the masses will react by oppressive measures and thereby reconfirm the *status quo*.[18]

The rebellious "no" of the first group gets stuck in the situated character of its negative activity, the anarchistic "no" of the second group loses sight of its situated character and becomes self-estranged in idealistic speculations, but the utopian "no" endeavors to "sublate" this opposition. Its critical negativity is inspired by the hope for, and trust in a better future. The utopian "nihilation" presupposes a more fundamental "yes" to the future in this sense: although the negation is an essential aspect of human freedom, it is this only as the counterpart and sign of a more fundamental possibility. The dialectical negation doesn't wish to "nihilate" or destroy the existing reality but to distantiate itself from it in order to experience its relativity and imperfection. Its antithetical attitude produces in the ossified and one-dimensional reality a certain "decompression of being," a leeway for new possibilities.

The utopian impetus doesn't merely wish nihilistically to "nihilate" the existing order or idealistically to demolish it in favor of a speculative future. The imagination creatively wants to bring to consciousness certain tendencies which are already alive below the surface. It brings to light the horizon of meaning which still lies repressed in the semidarkness of the unconscious. This is the more positive aspect of the utopia, but it is one which is always essentially connected with the negative aspect. The implicit "knowing" about the horizon of meaning, the normative "nowhere" is concretely pictured by the utopian imagination. That's why the term *utopia*, "nowhere" or "no-man's land" is used. The imagination places the human background on the foreground. Its description doesn't have the rational exactness of prognosis and planning, but the imagination fills the gaps in man's explicit knowledge.

Critical negativity and critical positivity imply each other. The utopian critique has an ironic character because it wishes to stimulate society to place itself playfully at a distance from what has already been accomplished and to relativize it. This utopian irony provokes freedom and constitutes "the great disturbance." In this way it functions as the catalyzer in a process of change that is radically humanizing.

12. The Utopia as Horizon Projected by Man

Society asks about the meaning and ultimate value of the technical-industrial order which, in a kind of Sartrian counter-finality, turns against man. Every system needs a goal which transcends the immanent laws governing its continuation. Because the hypertrophia of the culture of means practised by the consumer society threatens to obscure the final values, there is a growing need for a "horizon of planning."[1]

The rehabilitation of utopian thinking is connected not only with the question about the different values of technico-rational activities, but also and especially with the problem of how these different values can be harmonized. Our time needs not only the partial analyses that continue to increase today but also and even more a total synthesis. According to Mannheim, we need a "planning of planners." The radical intervention of the sciences in life has created a need for an overarching perspective, in the light of which society can determine its orientation and development in a responsible fashion. Two reasons need to be mentioned in connection with this need.

The first lies in the artificial isolation of the modern sciences with their specialization. This specialization leads to important discoveries in particular realms of human knowledge. The new discoveries often have profound effects on other realms of life, but these effects lie outside the scope of the particular science in question. Examples are offered by all kinds of chemical and technical inventions or discoveries, with respect to which insufficient attention has been paid to their side-effects on public health. Similarly, one can be a specialist in the theory of international trade and calculate exactly how the comparative cost differences lead to economic benefits for all participants. All this can be done "expertly," without any attention to the fact that so-called rational economic activities contain a great deal of irrationality and immorality with respect to certain countries. G. Picht sketches this development of science in the following way: "The science of the technological era is based on the systematic isolation of particular sets of phenomena. The network of interdependent relationships is cut to pieces and factors disturbing the set are left out."[2] The danger of professional idiocy and professional blindness exists in modern science if the professional expertise is not orientated to, and guided from within by, a background of values established in a democratic fashion. The overall process of social development is in danger of assuming the character of a blind fate through such isolated and one-sided expertise.

The second reason why especially today society needs an integrating perspective on the future lies in the enormous influence and dominating character of modern science. Scientific research produces all kinds of instruments for guiding nature, man and society, but it is not clear in what direction they must be guided. The increasing power to foresee and plan the future enlarges the scope of human possibilities. But which future possibilities should society select and to which values should it assign priority? Too many decisions are made in the dark, and society is dragged along by its own breakneck speed. A freedom which surrenders to its own unlimited possibilities without a sense of direction and meaning unchains blind forces.

Hitherto too little attention has been paid to the over-all process of social change. The social evolution in its totality is irrationally viewed as an inescapable fate or process of nature. This leads to an ever-increasing distance between the irrationality of life as a whole and the rationality characterizing particular sectors. The increasing rationality of the means to guide thus is put into the service of the irrationality of the goals, and this irrationality is on the increase. For the mere adding of partial rationalities doesn't automatically lead to an ideal totality.

This disharmonious development of the parts and this unguided increase of the means leads to unhealthy distortions and irrational waste. For example, the production of goods which will quickly wear out is defended on the ground that it is necessary to let the modern means of production grow bigger. Our rational economy develops into a system of planned obsolescences. Prosperous nations pour millions of dollars into underdeveloped countries, but at the same time drain off even greater sums in the form of profits produced by their economic rationality. Underdeveloped countries are helped to develop economically, but at the same time rational nationalistic reasons create stiff tariffs to offer protection against imports from these countries. Similarly, from the standpoint of self-defense rational arguments can perhaps be put forward for any country's armement against other countries, but at the same time this rationality leads to an irrational arms race throughout the world.

Its own specialistic expertise threatens to let society sink into a

situation where it has no control over itself. With respect to over-
all social organization people are as powerless as a worker is with
respect to a complex piece of machinery which has stalled. Social
politics is too much concerned with merely reforming the existing
structure and with matters of detail; it merely overhauls the machine and repairs whatever defects occur. Its future task, however
doesn't lie in the preservation of the existing order but in the building of a new order. The growing range of man's power demands an
orientating synthesis to prevent the developments occurring in the
various parts from destroying the totality through chaos.

The social feeling of being ill at ease in Eastern and Western
Europe, as well as in America, is the result of the revisionistic character of these political systems. Today's capitalistic and Marxist
systems differ only insofar as they voice preference for reform of
certain details within the same worn-out framework. Economical-
political life lacks the inspiration of a constructive over-all vision,
in which world peace, world solidarity and the personalization and
socialization of human relationships function as harmonizing values. Only a utopian vision which neither remains a vacuous dream
nor gets mired in the description of existing facts can inspire mankind to a common future task and save it from the present impasse.

As Bloch rightly says, "The concrete utopia stands at the horizon
of all reality."[3] He views the utopia as the harmonizing and orientating horizon of human and social reality. The horizon is indeed
connected with direction, meaning and orentation. On the one hand,
it circumscribes the reach of man, on the other, it opens a perspective on going forward without limit. The ambiguity of the horizon
lies precisely in this that it is both enclosing and disclosing, that
it limits and can be transcended. The far horizon is the point where
the limited and the unlimited intersect.

The horizon of vision helps society orientate itself within the
reality encompassed by it. The horizon is the *totum*, the overarching whole which integrates all perspectives into a meaningful totality. It is the harmonizing power which gives to the parts value in
reference to the whole. The horizon's consistency guarantees the
identity of man and society. Without this enclosing aspect of the

horizon human activities would disintegrate in chaos. At the same time, however, the horizon as enclosing has a disclosing aspect, and as far horizon points in the direction of invisible distances. Without the horizon society and human life would be dying or dead, but the horizon makes them pregnant again with new possibilities.

The utopian view has all the aspects of the horizon. Its picture of the future has the features of a far horizon, which both entices man to unknown distant lands and gives meaning and orientation to him in this adventure. The totalizing and integrating aspect of the horizon finds its expression in the "utopian concrete *totum*."[4] The classical utopia in particular expresses the harmonious unity and totality of the horizon of vision in a wealth of fantasy. It represents the utopian world as a "closed universe," even as an "insular little world."[5] Thomas More, for example, very originally expresses the ambiguity of horizon and distance, of enclosing and disclosing, of inside and outside. On the one hand he locates the utopian autarkic realm on an island, beyond the continent of human imperfections, but on the other, this island is situated just beyond the shore and thus still within reach of man. There is no better way of concretely representing the ambiguity of the horizon which is both within and outside our reach.

The utopian fantasy somewhat resembles Baron von Münchhausen's famous *tour de force* when he seized his hair to pull himself out of a swamp. "Every moment" counts for the utopian fantasy, "both in the things and outside them."[6] To cling to things is just as wrong as to disregard them. The imagination creates a vision of society, and this vision raises the level of society. It is also the organizing principle and the frame of reference of the various sciences. For the horizon combines the different perspectives from within into a structural whole. In this way it unfolds the implicit goals of scientific pursuits. It is at "every moment in the things." But the vision is not encompassed by them, it does not merely enclose but also discloses. The vision is not merely interested in filling a field of possibilities with imaginative contents but also in disclosing the field itself—which is an activity that precedes all attempts to fill the field. The utopian power of imagination itself, which is presupposed by every visionary portrayal but not encompassed by it, is even less concerned with filling the field than with transcending it. It manifests not so much the desire for the fulfillment of particular needs as a nostalgia for the total fulfillment of man's whole being.

The critical or dialectical pursuit of science deserves great praise for having emphasized the historical and social totality within which the various parts receive their meaning and direction. This totality is the context containing also the value elements which alone make it possible to interpret facts. Critical thinking wishes to understand the parts in the light of the whole, but also the whole in terms of the parts. Scientific analysis must be made in the light of social synthesis, but the social synthesis must also be scientifically analyzed. The reproach which critical thinking addresses to the neo-positivistic pursuit of science is that it limits itself to a non-totalized analysis. Without this totalizing dimension the specialization of the sciences produces only fragmentary quantitative results and doesn't make it possible for man to orientate himself better in society.

The advantage of critical thinking lies in the power of its synthetical approach. The empirical social sciences have devoted too little attention to society in its totality and its historical development. But the undeniable advantages of dialectical thought are accompanied by disadvantages. The synthetizing power of thought can easily change into a kind of syncretism or eclecticism. The attempt to proceed from the standpoint of a "whole" can result in simply positing such a whole in a more or less arbitrary fashion. The synthetizing character of the critical theory then assumes violent features. It forces the empirical material it has gathered into the services of its conceived "whole" without observing the characteristic prudence of science. The arbitrary whole distorts all details. The glory of the dialectical method then becomes its ignominy. A fully reified dialectics becomes undialectical.[7]

The reality of the totality is commensurate with the human horizon envisioned in this totality. But the problem is to determine how this horizon of meaning arises and how it is known. Many think that the dialectical process between the whole and the parts, and, conversely, between the parts and the whole—the dialectics of figure and horizon—occurs wholly on the scientific level; in other words, they think that the whole can be just as scientifically known as the parts. This is what H. Albert calls "the myth of total reason."[8] It is at this point that the dialectical pursuit of science can degenerate into dogmatism.

The horizon appears in the figure as a present absence. The horizon is not known by a scientific but by an imaginative perception, and the latter draws on both scientific understanding and creative fantasy. The horizon appears in the figure and thus can be perceived. But as a far horizon, it cannot possibly be reduced to the figure. Thus it lies beyond the reach of scientific perception, but not that of imaginative perception. It is this imaginative perception which offers a "vision" of the whole. This vision or totality is not an affirmative but a critical category.[9] Science ought to observe and affirm the facts in the light of this vision but this light does not belong to science itself. A total vision cannot be fully "translated" into the rationality of science, nor can it be totally built up in a scientific way, not even by means of an interdisciplinary approach. The utopia is rational in the broad sense of "wise" and "humane"; scientific rationality, important as it is, is merely a limited aspect of such wisdom. By their power of control the sciences can teach us much about the future, but such values as human freedom and democratic choice transcend the realm within the reach of science. If thinking about the future were to be delegated to the sciences alone, man's future would be desolate. He would then simply have to adapt himself to the plan imposed by the sciences. A vision of a human future cannot do without the indispensable support of scientific expertise, but it encompasses more than the realm of science. The utopia without science is empty, but science without utopia is blind.

Dialectical thought is on the wrong track if it thinks that it can build up a scientific theory of the whole. It then commits a kind of eclecticism rather than the construction of a synthetizing new horizon. It is wrong to assign to the utopian over-all vision a scientific status. One who tries to do this is unfaithful to the dialectical process and lapses into a new kind of neo-positivism—the kind that is not concerned with the parts but with the whole. The critical theory recognizes that there exists a dialectical process between scientific analysis and utopian synthesis, but not one between scientific analysis and scientific synthesis. The pursuit of science without synthetical vision leads to the chaos of independently developed parts, but pursuing science in the light of an assumed scientific knowledge of the totality leads to ideological dogmatism and frightful simplifications, it results in a kind of "theology" of society. Popper is right when he vigorously opposes this sort of holistic thought, this kind of historicism.

The neo-Marxist Adorno acknowledges that positivism has helped dialectical thought in abstaining from assigning the inflexible character of a system to the essence, that is to say, the totality. The totality is a historical whole in the process of becoming, not a whole that can be fixed as a fact or a thing. The whole is criticized "in its own contradiction, i.e., insofar as it stands in contrast to 'what appears' and ultimately to the real life of each man individually."[10]

All this has consequences also for the renewal of society. A better society will not come about by an approach directed only to parts and details. Such a procedure is nothing but a "reformistic" tuning of an existing machine. Similarly, it is meaningless to create at once a new totality without the appropriate parts. Only an interconnected whole of reforms in the light of a utopian vision, a strategic plan aimed at a goal, will set the process of radical changes into motion.[11]

There is much talk in our Western world about revolution. If this term is supposed to refer to an all-encompassing and radically different horizon of the future, then the use of this term is undoubtedly correct. But if it is taken to mean that the new society can be brought about by the sudden overthrow of the existing situation by a minority, it shows a lack of critical sense. First of all, one goes then against the revolution's own goals. Only a conscious guidance of the socio-economic development on a democratic basis from the bottom up can lead to a better man and a better form of society. An educational dictatorship by a minority is hardly suitable for such a purpose. Secondly, the complex technico-economic substructure, on which the possible enlargement and satisfaction of true human needs is based, is subjected to utter chaos and destruction by an abrupt charge. A socialistic and democratic society is possible only on the basis of a highly developed technical level of production. Marx himself was clever enough to see this point.

Marxism deserves credit for emphasizing the interconnection between social phenomena. But this strong point has often also become its weak point. All too readily Marxism believes that it alone is in possession of the true—and even scientific—knowledge of the totality. The utopian horizon, however, can always only be approached from a certain perspective, that is to say, one cannot look at the totality from all sides at the same time. The various perspectives together offer a better vision of the whole. The parliamentary democracy fundamentally starts from this idea and wishes to attain a better society through the different perspectives presented by the system of political parties. But Marcuse is right when he says that parliamentary democracy today is largely paralyzed and unable to function. The reason is that, on the one hand, the national democratic power is no longer able to cope with international economic power, and on the other, the parliament is estranged from its basis, the voters. But it would be wrong to toss out the baby with the bathwater. What we need is a further democratization on the basic level and a parliamentary democracy on a world-wide level. Democracy needs to be deepened at the foundation and broadened at the top.

Marcuse's suggestion that provisionally it can be left to an intellectual elite to assume leadership[12] is based on the previously mentioned faulty presupposition that the vision of the future is primarily a matter of scientific rationality and expertise. Marcuse falls here into the very trap of technical rationality which he is busily fighting against. His suggestion would mean giving up the achievements of the French Revolution. If an intellectual elite thinks that its perspective on the totality is the only right one, it thinks one-dimensionally. The danger of repression recurs here, but now in the form of intolerance. One who thinks that he has the right view available for the others makes it very difficult to have a liberating communication. He who strives for the utopian future wants as many people as possible to walk the road to greater freedom of their own free will. He will proceed radically against unfreedom but he will not use unfreedom as a means to educate people to freedom. Marcuse's confidence in the power position of an intellectual elite is difficult to defend. If one assumes that the present power elite will not voluntarily give up its position, on what basis can one be confident that the revolutionary intellectuals will do so voluntarily? Such an assumption is gratuitous, unless one thinks that there are two kinds of people, the good and the bad, and that intellectuals belong to the first kind.

13.   VALUE-FREE CRITICAL SOCIAL SCIENCES

The revival of utopian thought is closely connected with the call for critical social science. The accusation addressed to the existing sciences is that they do not sufficiently assume a critical attitude with respect to society, which as the overarching totality permeates all elements.

At first, such an accusation seems to be a paradox. In the Modern Era the sciences were able to develop precisely because they abandoned the existing medieval pattern of values. It was the positive sciences which broke through the medieval overarching view of life and the world. Precisely in the medieval civilization it was true that knowledge of parts and details was incorporated into the overall knowledge of the totality. Every particular phenomenon, such as disastrous floods or illness, was interpreted in a biblical-theological fashion in the light of the medieval worldview. The positive sciences began to flourish in our Western civilization because they addressed themselves to the observation of details, divorced from the overarching totality of the worldview. The Galileo affair is a clear-cut example of this. When Galileo claimed that the earth orbited round the sun, he acted as a man of science, that is to say, on the basis of what he perceived with his telescope and could calculate mathematically. The rebuttal of the medieval-minded authorities was not that he had made erroneous calculations about what he had seen. No, they knew from their biblically-inspired worldview that things were different and they didn't even want to look through a telescope. If Galileo and many others had not liberated themselves in their observations from the existing values, the valuable positive sciences would never have been born. Thus "value-free" science is indeed itself a "value."

The Enlightenment rightly insisted on a value-free and objective approach. Enlightened thinking justly stripped itself of all prejudices arising from a metaphysical and religious worldview, which from without and from above imposed value-judgments on scientific research. To be value-free meant then to be liberated from an authoritarian transcendent world-image. Science turned against belief on authority and "priestly deception." But the prejudice of the Enlightenment itself is the prejudice against all prejudices.[1] The Enlightenment tended to forget that it is actually impossible and not even desirable to liberate oneself from all values. Being value-free is only an abstraction, a thought construct, by means of which the man of research observes the part for a moment by itself, as if it were cut loose from the value which it has for the whole. In the real world, however, everything is connected with everything else. An item of knowledge discovered by man, such as the atomic theory, is of value for the whole of mankind. The Enlightenment also started implicitly from an over-all view of the totality. It assumed the existence of a given natural order which kept its own equilibrium. The "prejudice" of the Enlightened ideal of science was that of *laisser faire.*

From the preceding remarks it should be evident that the problem of value-free social science versus value-oriented or critical social science must be clarified by making certain necessary distinctions. A scientific mind which thinks that it can assume a neutral and value-free attitude with respect to the facts proceeds just as unrealistically as an approach for which those values are "written in heaven." If matters are conceived in such a way, the antinomy is faulty. Between values and science there must be a dialectical reciprocity in which both poles remain distinct but related to each other. Dialectics must not obscure either the unity of, nor the distinction between utopian ideal and hard reality. It is an essential point in a critical or dialectical theory that both values and science have a relative autonomy. Thus the critical theory defends, on the one hand, the critical core of science, and on the other, the scientific core of critique.[2] Let us examine both points.

With respect to the first point, *the critical core of science*, the critical theory distantiates itself from what it calls the traditional theory. M. Horkheimer in particular discusses this point extensively.[3] He holds that the traditional theory is based on the Cartesian split between subject and object, it starts from the autonomous and ahistorical subject and from the ahistorical object that is independent of man. Horkheimer rightly says that both the perceived object and the perceiving subject are historically and socially determined. But his picture of the traditional theory is somewhat simplistic because of the contrasting light he throws on the opposing theories. Even Weber, who symbolizes the ideology of value-free science, holds that sociology is connected with values in the selection of its problems and the determination of its concepts.[4]

The difference between the hermeneutics of the Enlightenment and that of our time can be more truthfully expressed as follows. Enlightened thinking wanted to "bracket" and neutralize the "*Sitz im Leben*," the framework of one's own life situation. Contemporary hermeneutics, on the other hand, precisely wishes to take into account how man looks at the world today and wants to start from a background of values. Man may and must start from presuppositions, but he should do so consciously and critically. In this respect, then, it would be better to speak of consciousness of, rather than freedom from values.

Accordingly, the emphasis on the critical core of science implies that there must be a democratic dialogue between science and society at large. The scientist must ask himself whether the values by which he is guided in the selection of his problems and the values for which the results of his science can be used are in harmony with the values of life desired by society in a truly democratic dialogue. It is not up to the scientist here to say the last word. In determining what is "rational" for society as a whole, it is not enough to have scientific rationality. "Rational" should be understood here in the enlarged sense of human and humane. Only a democratic core-sponsibility for the selection of problems and the application of the results achieved by science offers the best possible guarantee for this rationality. Scientific expertise as such cannot present any special credentials with respect to this rationality in the enlarged sense.

In this way the critical core of science emphasizes, on the one hand, that scientific autonomy is only relative. Science is dependent on values outside science. On the other hand, it is also emphasized that values possess a certain autonomy with respect to science. Ethical and political rationality cannot be reduced to scientific rationality. In this matter a certain rehabilitation is due to Max Weber, who is so often disparaged by the critical theory. Undoubtedly it is true that Weber overemphasized the autonomy of science and thus accentuated the split between values and science. But his concern for making science value-free was really inspired by an even greater concern for keeping values science-free. What Weber wished more than anything else was that political and ethical autonomy would not perish in the one-dimensional rationality of science.[5]

The critical theory also argues in favor of *the scientific core of critique*. Habermas, for example, wishes to show, on the one hand, that the analytical conception of science and the current sociology are ideologically determined, but on the other hand, he also recognizes that there is a progressive and humane element in the critical aspirations of science itself.[6] One who assumes a critical social attitude can still proceed very uncritically from the standpoint of science. According to Habermas, the Marxist dialectical theory actually sometimes proceeds either light-heartedly or dogmatically insofar as the empirical-scientific content of critique is concerned.

The scientific core of critique demands that scientific criteria be observed in the investigation. These criteria are, first, the logical precision and consistency of the theory itself, in virtue of which all scientific statements can be understood by every man of science in the same sense; secondly, the exactness of the analysis, in virtue of which the empirical statements, obtained from a value-selective standpoint, can be acknowledged as true and verified by every observer, even if he doesn't share the same pattern of values. This form of scientific objectivity, of being value-free, is itself a value. The values involved here are values internal to science.

The empirical truth of the value judgments will have to be investigated and registered in scientific analysis. That's why it is scientifically unjustifiable to obscure from a certain normative standpoint certain facts which fall within one's perspective and to overemphasize others. Undoubtedly different normative standpoints are possible, but within any standpoint one must proceed in a logically consistent way and do justice to the empirical phenomena which present themselves within the field of vision. In this respect the "normative power of what actually is" retains its validity.

Thus one goes against the value-free character of science, or rather its empirical value, if one handles values as premises and deduces empirical statements from them as conclusions. He who uses the principle of freedom from value in such a way opens up a Pandora box of evils in the world of science. The most terrifying example of this was Hitler's Nazi-Germany, which permitted only the pursuit of Aryan physics and biology. And in the U.S.S.R. also the development of physics was impaired when this science had to be pursued along Marxist lines.

As O. Duintjer rightly remarks, "The fact that a scientific inquiry is guided by selective viewpoints which are inspired by social values is not formally the same as making these values normative. As far as the inquiry is concerned, these values can be given a hypothetical status."[7] The fact that values function as a background of scientific research is a positive good, provided one remains critically conscious of these normative presuppositions.

Such a critical consciousness means, first of all, that the values must also be tested for their empirical truth. A theoretical knowledge, based on carefully checked data, assists in conforming or purifying the current pattern of values. Secondly, a critical attitude toward normative presuppositions demands that one remain conscious of the limitations and restrictions inherent in the empirical knowledge acquired from such a selective standpoint. One will then be open to research based on different value backgrounds and be ready to collaborate in an immediate discussion of values on a truly democratic level. On the other hand, it is entirely irresponsible to conclude from values as premises alone that other scientific theories are scientifically false, for scientific theories must be confirmed or refuted on the basis of empirical knowledge.[8]

Accordingly, the scientific core of the critical theory confirms that values have only a relative autonomy. The discussion of values must not be left to philosophers or politicians alone, for science also has a contribution to make. The critical theory differs in this respect from Weber's view. Weber was willing to let science be aware of ethical presuppositions, but only in order to establish the inner limitations of the scientific inquiry. He did not think that science can make a contribution to the question whether the values from which the empirical investigation is started are in harmony with the genuine values of well-being and happiness. For Weber values were a matter of subjective taste, about which one cannot argue.

Because the scientific core of the critical theory emphasizes that values have only a relative autonomy, it assigns at the same time a measure of autonomy, of freedom from value, to science. Science is bound up with ethical, political and cultural values, with values said to be external to science, but at the same time science must also respect its own values, the vaues internal to it.

Many terminological confusions occur in the problem of value-free versus value-conscious science. For example, the New Left declares that in the 1930s the principle of value-free science caused the German universities to offer little or no resistance to Nazism. The New Left is against freedom from value and argues in favor of "politicizing" science. On the other hand, precisely the academic advocates of Nazism in the 1930s defended the idea that science ought to be politicized. For example, the Nazi professor E. Krieck said at that time that "political" science should replace "value-free" science.[9] But the prominent jurist Hans Kelsen, who sharply opposed Nazism, appealed precisely to the value-free character of science to resist the Nazi efforts to politicize science.[10]

What is happening here is that two generations are speaking a different language. Students do not believe in the value-free character of science and demand that the university be politicized, while their professors are allergic to such a move and fight for freedom from values. A purely terminological confusion causes much misunderstanding here. Because of their historical origin the terms "value-free" and "politicizing" are not very suitable to indicate the problem that is really involved in this controversy. As we saw, the term "value-free" dates from the Enlightenment and has mainly the negative meaning of liberation from ecclesiastical and political guardians. In this context to advocate freedom from value means to fight for the value of science. But in reaction to this authoritarian guardianship science tends to assume an attitude that is too neutral. That's why today the claim is rightly made that scientific research must also become conscious of its role as a critic of society. The term "freedom from values" with its negative meaning, no matter how justified it was in the authoritarian context of the Enlightenment, is less suitable in our time. Today it would be better to speak of value-consciousness. Science should be conscious of both its own scientific value and its social value. The term "politicizing" with its dismal recent past, on the other hand, is entirely unsuitable for expressing the social involvement of science. "Politicizing science" evokes the frightening image of an intolerant political ideology which keeps science in chains. Such a term, therefore, should be avoided and replaced by "critique of society."

One who wishes to defend genuine values must first of all see to it that he expresses his intentions in clear language. The terms "freedom from value" and "politicizing" do not possess such clarity. One party mounts the barricades as soon as it hears the words "freedom from values," while the other party begins to fortify its defenses as soon as the term "politicizing" is used. The critical theory calls on science to become socially involved and pursue the critique of society. History teaches us that science in its commitment to neutrality has often unwittingly served social injustice and oppression. The critical theory with its scientific core demands constant willingness to be self-critical and to carefully investigate the facts. Here, again, history can teach us a lesson. Many scientists and scholars, serving an authoritarian political regime, have been unscrupulous with respect to scientific truth and did not hesitate to collaborate in such crimes as genocide. On the other hand, a critique of society which does not appreciate logically consistent and empirical verification is just as unsuitable and as dangerous as a science which neglects to inquire into the social value of its activity.

The reproach that in the recent past the sciences have assumed an insufficiently critical attitude toward society is justified. But there exists now a danger of going too far in the opposite direction. Today society is often criticized in a superficial way, without any attempt to make an accurate analysis of the phenomena. All kinds of assertions are glibly made and supported by a number of haphazard examples. A scientific analysis obviously demands much more than this. It requires a careful formulation of the different hypotheses, a stringent development of the conceptual apparatus, an exact gathering of the data and a prudent formulation of conclusions. All this demands solid training.

Far too often critique of society is based on nebulous metaphysical "essences." If these essences, moreover, are dressed in Marxist garments, their truth is held to be *a priori* guaranteed. Without bothering to arrive at a clear description of what is meant, people glibly speak of "the reign of necessity" and "the reign of freedom," false and true needs, manipulation and freedom, alienation and authentic consciousness. Next, they use these vague concepts as premises from which they can draw conclusions about empirical phenomena, without going to the trouble of making an exact analysis.[11]

The critique of society demands not only a scientific asceticism but also unremitting self-critique. A healthy consciousness of the world is only possible if one has a healthy self-consciousness, and vice versa. This is why critique of society without conscious self-critique easily leads to the prejudiced standpoint where one says: society is wrong and, since I am critical of society, I am on the right side. Critique of society, one should not forget, is also self-critique because I am part of society. For example, it is very easy for me to fight for greater equalization of income as long as it doesn't mean that my salary is reduced. On the other hand, it is a valuable gain that today emphasis is put on the fact that society is the totality which permeates all elements. If, however, the critique of society is not to become a hollow phrase devoid of meaning, then it demands that the elements be approached in a careful analytic way.

14. Concluding Considerations

"What today is a utopia, tomorrow can become a reality." This believing trust of man in his own future is the principle and source of all utopian thinking. Like the fairy tale, the utopia has always known wishful dreams, but instead of saying, "once upon a time there was," it says, "there will be a time when." The accomplishments of science and technology have made the future more and more a project of man's own power. Today man's power of control makes the future a land of unlimited possibilities, but also a realm of dark threats. Human existence, which through the power of technological development is more than ever "ahead of itself," is infrastructurally in a state of permanent revolution. Because the stormy developments are not accompanied and guided superstructurally by a continuing education, they threaten to turn against society itself in a kind of blind automatic reaction and to lead to a cultural chaos. The crisis in which our society lives today is unique in history. Western Europe has gone through many critical situations in the past, but these crises were struggles of the future against the past. For example, the Renaissance was a time when a new self-consciousness of man tried to break through and thus revolted against the mysticism of the medieval world. But the distinguishing feature of our crisis situation is that we face the humanization and domination of the future, which comes over us as a blind destiny. Our crisis does not so much demand that we distantiate ourselves from the past as that we humanize a power over the future which we ourselves have already unchained. Our time must learn to shape the future in a humane manner.

In every social crisis, as in any serious illness, there is a critical point which decides between life or death, the return to health or lethal degeneration. Some people are pessimistic about our situation, and this also happens whenever there is a critical stage. They ask themselves whether a return to health is still possible in a welfare state where everything is connected with everything else. Wouldn't a revolution in a technically highly developed culture result in self-destruction?[1] Isn't the only remedy left to use pain-killing means which can camouflage and delay the process of decomposition?

Some people live in a kind of anti-utopian mood, which is connected with Sigmund Freud's views of culture. According to Freud, civilization is essentially restrictive and repressive. With his pleasure principle man remains fundamentally an enemy of civilization and its principle of reality. To the extent that civilization increases and imposes more and more prohibitions, the destruction created by the death-instinct becomes greater. Will not man ultimately prefer completely to destroy the civilization which he experiences as a prison rather than interiorize it? Although it is not necessary to adopt such a pessimistic anti-utopian attitude, the view contains a sober warning. It puts revolutionaries on the alert not to speak too poetically of violent revolution and warns conservatives not to aggravate their provocations of the power to destroy by unyielding reactionary steps.

Fortunately most people remain optimistic and utopically express their hope in a new future. The utopia has always known the wishful dream about ultimate unity and reconciliation. But does this remain a mere wish for man or will he eventually be able to accomplish this hope? The utopia has always inspired people with the power of hope for further discovery and improvement of the world. The far horizon points out that man's power is essentially without circumscribed limits. But philosophically and theologically the question must be asked whether precisely in this future coming from man, the Future is coming to man. Does the utopian *novum* involve an eschatological *novissimum*? Is the Infinite the source of the progression without limit of human freedom? Does the Kingdom appear in the utopia, the *Kairos* in *chronos*?[2] Is the "principle of hope" based on the theology of hope?[3]

The Marxist trend of thought firmly believes in the possibility of an ideal self-realization by mankind in the world. Its utopia lives by the expectation that man's fractured existence will ultimately be overcome on earth by man himself. Its wish-dream is that the split between man's present condition and his non-present "essence" will eventually be healed. Marx speaks of the "reign of freedom" where nature will be humanized and man will be naturalized. Marxism puts great trust in a grand ideal. According to Marcuse, "the end of utopia" is possible in the form of an "existence that has found peace." Habermas believes in the "dialogue of all with all, free of all domination." Bloch hopes for "the fatherland of identity."

For the Marxist the future is nothing but the future of the still-concealed man and the still-concealed world. The Christian with his certainty of divine salvation too easily resigns himself to the imperfect conditions of life. Because God's kingdom is guaranteed for the Christian, says the Marxist, human history remains an unimportant dimension. Christian understanding of reality, on the other hand, sees Marxism as an overwrought expectation of the empirical subject, which is dialectically changed again into an ironclad necessity of history.[4] For the Christian, the Marxist doesn't sufficiently pay attention to history as an "event" and easily resorts to filling the open future with messianic utopias.

Christianity can learn from Marxism that serving God is accomplished by serving the world. The Marxist utopia of the totality of world history must be for the Christian man's way of giving form to the hope and the desire for the promised kingdom of God and its freedom. But will Christ's promise, "Behold, I make everything new," break open the dialectical immanent process of the world with its "transcending without transcendence"? Does Christ's promise give an even more profound background to the utopian horizon of harmony and reconciliation between mankind and nature? Does the utopian hope become an even better founded expectation because working and laboring man changes history while serving the forces of Reconciliation?

Notes—Part One

CHAPTER 1

[1] K. Keniston, *Young Radicals. Notes on Committed Youth*, New York, 1968; G. Mendel, *La révolte contre le père*, Paris, 1968; *La crise des générations*, Paris, 1969.

CHAPTER 2

[1] J. van Santen, "Economische critiek en dialectiek," *Economie*, vol. 34, 1970, pp. 345 ff.; J. K. Galbraith, *The New Industrial State*, New York, 1968.

[2] H. Marcuse, *One-dimensional Man*, Boston, 1964; *Eros and Civilization*, Boston, 1955; *An Essay on Liberation*, London, 1969.

[3] R. Beerling, "Doelen en middelen," *Mens en Maatschappij*, vol. 28, Jan.-Feb., 1968, pp. 13 ff.

[4] J. Henry, *Culture Against Man*, New York, 1965, p. 25.

[5] E. Levinas, *Totality and Infinity*, Pittsburgh, Pa., 1969.

[6] J. Metz, *Zur Theologie der Welt*, München, 1968, pp. 100 ff.

[7] R. Koselleck, *Kritik und Krise. Ein Beitrag zur Pathogenese der bürgerlichen Welt*, Freiburg, 1959.

[8] M. Plattel, "Op weg naar een nieuwe wereld," *Intermediair*, vol. 5, April 25, 1969, pp. 77 ff.

[9] A. Dekker, "Geweld en recht," *Tijdschrift voor Filosofie*, vol. 30, 1968, pp. 675 ff.

CHAPTER 3

[1] F. Polak, *De toekomst is verleden tijd*, Part Two, Utrecht, 1955, p. 331. English edition, *The Image of the Future*, New York, 1961.

[2] F. Polak, *Prognostica, Wordende wetenschap schouwt en schept de toekomst*, Part Two, Deventer, 1968, pp. 28 ff.

[3] R. Ruyer, *L'utopie et les utopies*, Paris, 1950, pp. 4 f.

[4] E. Bloch, *Das Prinzip Hoffnung*, 3 vols., Frankfurt a.M., 1967. English ed., *The Principle of Hope*, to be published by Herder and Herder, New York, 1972.

[5] L. Kofler, *Der asketische Eros. Industriekultur und Ideologie*, Vienna, 1967.

[6] R.Ruyer, *op. cit.*, pp. 9 ff.

[7] P. Tillich, *Die politische Bedeutung der Utopie im Leben der Völker*, Berlin, 1957, pp. 8 f.

[8] H. Plessner, *Die Stufen des Organischen und der Mensch*, Berlin, 1965, p. 343.

[9] D. Riesman, "Some Observations on Community Plans and Utopia," *The Yale Law Journal*, vol. 57, 1947, pp. 174 ff.

[10] C. W. Wright Mills, *The Sociological Imagination*, New York, 1959.

[11] R. Jungk, "De sociale fantasie," *Euros*, 1967, No. 1, p. 33.

[12] E. Bloch, *Subjekt-Objekt. Erläuterungen zu Hegel*, Frankfurt a.M., 1962, pp. 462 and 470.

[13] L. Kolakowski, *Der Mensch ohne Alternative*, München, 1956. (p. 133 in Dutch edition).

CHAPTER 4

[1] For the history of utopian thought see the above-mentioned works of F. Polak, *De toekomst is verleden tijd*; E. Bloch, *Das Prinzip Hoffnung*, pp. 547-929; and also M. Schwonke, *Vom Staatsroman zur Science Fiction*, Stuttgart, 1957.

[2] F. Polak, *op. cit.*, pp. 46 ff.   [3] F. Polak, *op. cit.*, pp. 129 ff.

[4] M. Schwonke, *op. cit.*, p. 1.

[5] R. Ruyer, *L'utopie et les utopies*, pp. 187 ff.

[6] F. Polak, *op. cit.*, pp. 170 ff.

[7] M. Schwonke, *op. cit.*, pp. 92 ff.

[8] H. Klages, *Soziologie zwischen Wirklichkeit und Möglichkeit*, Köln, 1968, pp. 19 ff.

[9] F. Polak, *op. cit.*, pp. 268 ff.   [10] H. Klages, *op. cit.*, pp. 35 ff.

[11] F. Polak, *op. cit.*, p. 273.

[12] O. Duintjer, "Moderne wetenschap en waardevrijheid," *Alg. Nederlands Tijdschrift voor wijsbegeerte*, vol. 62, 1970, p. 37.

[13] D. Riesman, *art. cit.*, p. 179.

[14] G. Picht, *Prognose, Utopie, Planung, Die Situation des Menschen in der Zukunft der technischen Welt*, Stuttgart, 1967.

[15] M. Mead, "Towards More Vivid Utopias," *Science*, Nov. 8, 1957, pp. 957 ff.

[16] B. van Steenbergen, *Orde of Conflict*, Hilversum, 1969.

[17] G. Picht, *op. cit.*, pp. 13 ff.

[18] H. Klages, *op. cit.*, pp. 35 ff.

[19] Th. Adorno, *Negative Dialektik*, Frankfurt a.M., 1966. English ed., *Negative Dialectics*, New York, 1971.

[20] L. Kolakowski, *op. cit.*, p. 132.

[21] H. Marcuse, *Das Ende der Utopie*, Berlin, 1967, p. 20.

[22] Kolakowski, *op. cit.*, p. 134.

CHAPTER 5

[1] "Utopian societies are monolithic, homogeneous edifices, which float freely not only in time but also in space, cut off from the external world, for the latter can always become a threat to the highly-praised immobility of their social structure." R. Dahrendorf, *Pfade aus Utopia*, München, 1967, p. 246.

[2] A. Neusüss, *Utopie. Begriff und Phenomen des Utopischen*, Neuwied, 1968, pp. 18 ff.

[3] E. Bloch, *op. cit.*, p. 14.

[4] K. Mannheim, "Utopia," *Encyclopedia of the Social Sciences*, ed. 1935, vol. XV, p. 201.

[5] A. Lalande, *Vocabulaire technique et critique de la philosophie*, Paris, 1928, p. 934.

[6] A. Neusüss, *op. cit.*, p. 31.

CHAPTER 6

[1] Transcendental doesn't mean the same as transcendent. The transcendent refers to another world beyond this world, but the transcendental indicates the elementary structures of this world.

² F. Baumer, *Paradiese der Zukunft. Die Menschheitsträume vom besseren Leben,* München, 1967. Quoted after the Dutch edition, pp. 53 ff.

³ L. Kofler, *op. cit.,* p. 34.

⁴ L. Kofler, *op. cit.,* p. 319.

⁵ E. Bloch, *op. cit.,* pp. 161 ff.

⁶ E. Bloch, *op. cit.,* p. 166.

CHAPTER 7

¹ E. Bloch, *Philosophische Grundfragen,* vol. 1, Frankfurt a.M., 1961, p. 65.

² H. Marcuse, *Reason and Revolution,* New York, 1963, pp. 152 ff.

CHAPTER 8

¹ R. Ruyer, *op. cit.,* pp. 5 ff.

² W. Banning, *Moderne maatschappijproblemen,* Haarlem, 1953, pp. 110 ff.

³ F. Polak, *op. cit.,* pp. 304 ff.

⁴ K. Popper, *The Poverty of Historicism,* London, 1967.

⁵ H. Albert, "Der Mythos der totalen Vernunft," *Der Positivismusstreit in der deutschen Soziologie,* Neuwied, 1970, pp. 193 ff.

⁶ F. Polak, *op. cit.,* pp. 292 ff.

⁷ E. Bloch, *Das Prinzip Hoffnung,* p. 1625.

CHAPTER 9

¹ For the history of the concept "ideology" see H. Barth, *Wahrheit und Ideologie,* Zürich, 1945; K. Lenk, *Ideologie,* Neuwied, 1967; Th. Geiger, *Ideologie und Wahrheit,* Stuttgart, 1953; J. Barion, *Ideologie, Wissenschaft, Philosophie,* Bonn, 1966.

² K. Mannheim, *Ideologie und Utopie,* Frankfurt a.M., 1965, p. 66. English edition, *Ideology and Utopia,* New York, 1952.

³ E. Bloch, *op. cit.,* p. 174.

⁴ H. Barth, *op. cit.,* pp. 127 ff.

⁵ K. Lehmann, "De kerk en de heerschappij van de ideologien," *Kerk in de moderne samenleving. Handboek van de pastoraaltheologie,* vol. 4, Hilversum, 1968, pp. 100 ff.

⁶ K. Mannheim, *op. cit.,* pp. 229 ff.

⁷ K. Mannheim, *op. cit.,* pp. 242 ff.

⁸ R. Aron, "Fin de l'âge idéologique?", *Sociologica,* vol. 1, Frankfurt a.M., 1955, pp. 219 ff.

⁹ D. Bell, *The End of Ideology,* New York, 1965.

¹⁰ O. Brunner, "Das Zeitalter der Ideologien: Anfang und Ende," *Neue Wege der Sozialgeschichte,* Göttingen, 1956, pp. 194 ff.

¹¹ H. Schelsky, *Der Mensch in der wissenschaftlichen Zivilisation,* Köln, 1961.

¹² J. Habermas, *Technik und Wissenschaft als "Ideologie,"* Frankfurt a.M., 1969, pp. 120 ff.

¹³ D. Bell, *op. cit.,* pp. 405 ff.

¹⁴ M. Horkheimer and Th. Adorno, *Dialektik der Aufklärung,* Frankfurt a.M.,

1969; English ed., *Dialectic of Enlightenment*, New York, 1971; Horkheimer, *Kritische Theorie*, 2 vols., Frankfurt a.M., 1968.

15 J. Habermas, *Erkenntnis und Interesse*, Frankfurt a.M., 1968.

16 J. Habermas, *Technik und Wissenschaft als "Ideologie,"* pp. 88 ff.

17 H. Marcuse, *Kultur und Gesellschaft*, vol. 1, Frankfurt, a.M., pp. 56 ff.

18 Quoted after Lehmann, *op. cit.*, p. 106.

19 K. Mannheim, *op. cit.*, pp. 169 ff.

20 P. Thoenes, *Utopie en Ratio*, Meppel, 1969, p. 19.

21 J. Barion, *Was ist Ideologie?*, Bonn, 1964, pp. 24 ff.; R. Beerling, *Wijsgerig-sociologische verkenningen*, vol. 2, Arnhem, 1965, pp. 17 ff.

22 E. Bloch, *op. cit.*, p. 164.

23 E. Bloch, *op. cit.*, pp. 174 ff.

24 J. Hersch, *Die Ideologien und die Wirklichkeit*, München, 1957.

25 C. van Peursen, *Feiten, waarden, gebeurtenissen*, Amsterdam, 1965.

26 Quoted after K. Lehmann, *op. cit.*, p. 113.

27 K. Lehmann, *op. cit.*, p. 113.

CHAPTER 10

1 R. Ruyer, *op. cit.*, p. 12.

2 G. Picht, *Mut zur Utopie*, München, 1967.

3 E. Fischer, *Kunst und Koexistenz, Beitrag zu einer modernen marxistischen Aesthetik*, Hamburg, 1966, p. 182.

4 A. Mitscherlich, "De stad van de toekomst," *Katernen 2000*, May, 1970, p. 5.

5 L. Kolakowski, *op. cit.*, p. 134.

6 M. Plattel, "De filosofie van het spel en het spel van de filosofie," *Tijdschrift voor Filosofie*, vol. 29, 1967, pp. 281.

CHAPTER 11

1 W. Mündel, *Functie van de sociale utopie*, Amersfoort, n.d., pp. 85 ff.; H. J. Krymanski, "Die utopische Methode," *Dortmunder Schriften zur Sozialforschung*, vol. 21, Köln, 1963.

2 P. Ricoeur, "Prévision économique et choix éthique," *Esprit*, vol. 34, 1966, pp. 184 ff.

3 H. Plessner, quoted by M. Schwonke, *op. cit.*, p. 129.

4 R. Beerling, *op. cit.*, vol. 1, p. 92. E. Fink remarks: "With human playfulness, then, the over-all reality of real things and events is invaded by an 'unreal' sphere of meaning which is here and yet not here, now and yet not now." *Spiel als Weltsymbol*, Stuttgart, 1960, pp. 229 and 234.

5 Th. Adorno, *Negative Dialektik*, Frankfurt a.M., 1966.

6 K. Kosik, *Die Dialektik des Konkreten*, Frankfurt a.M., 1967.

7 A. Duyvendak, "Oefening in nee-zeggen," *Katernen 2000*, Feb., 1969.

8 Th. Elbert, "Buitenparlementaire oppositie," *ibid.*, p. 16.

9 Th. Adorno, "Zur Logik der Sozialwissenschaften," *Kölner Zeitschrift für Soziologie und Sozialpsychologie*, vol. 14, 1962, p. 262.

[10] L. Goldmann, "Kritiek op het negatieve van de negatieve dialectiek," *Dialectiek en maatschappijkritiek*, Meppel, 1970, pp. 88 ff.

[11] L. Goldmann, *art. cit.*, p. 89.

[12] L. Kofler, *op. cit.*, p. 314.

[13] A. Aron, *D'une sainte famille à l'autre*, Paris, 1970, pp. 31 ff.

[14] H. Holz, *Utopie und Anarchismus. Zur Kritik der kritischen Theorie Herbert Marcuses*, Köln, 1968, pp. 47 ff.

[15] H. Holz, *op. cit.*, pp. 116 ff.

[16] H. Holz, *op. cit.*, pp. 83 ff.

[17] L. Goldmann, *art. cit.*, p. 98.

[18] H. Holz, *op. cit.*, pp. 116 ff.

CHAPTER 12

[1] J. Domenach, "Note sur le bon usage de l'avenir," *Esprit*, vol. 34, 1960, p. 273.

[2] G. Picht, "Die Situation des Menschen in der Zukunft der technischen Welt," *Rundbrief der Vereinigung Deutscher Wissenschaftler*, no. 28, Dec., 1966. Quoted after A. Mitscherlich, *art. cit.*, p. 4.

[3] E. Bloch, *op. cit.*, p. 258.

[4] E. Bloch, *Subjekt-Objekt*, pp. 462 and 470.

[5] R. Ruyer, *op. cit.*, p. 25.

[6] Th. Adorno, *Minima Moralia*, Frankfurt a.M., 1951, p. 130; S. Buve, "Utopie als Kritik," *Säcularisation und Utopie. Erbracher Studien*, Stuttgart, 1967, p. 33.

[7] Th. Adorno, "Einleitung," *Der Positivismus in der deutschen Soziologie*, p. 35.

[8] H. Albert, "Der Mythos der totalen Vernunft," *ibid.*, pp. 193 ff.

[9] Th. Adorno, *loc. cit.* in footnote 7, p. 19.

[10] Th. Adorno, *ibid.*

[11] A. Gortz, *Le socialisme difficile*, Paris, 1967. Quoted after the Dutch edition, pp. 77 ff.

[12] H. Marcuse, *Versuch über die Befreiung*, Frankfurt a.M., 1969, pp. 104 ff.

CHAPTER 13

[1] H. Gadamer, *Wahrheit und Methode*, Tübingen, 1960, p. 255.

[2] A. Wellmer, *Kritische Gesellschaftstheorie und Positivismus*, Frankfurt a.M., 1969, p. 55.

[3] M. Horkheimer, *Kritische Theorie*, vol. 2, Frankfurt a.M., 1968, pp. 137 ff.

[4] J. Thurlings, "Het sociologische geweten," *Sociologische Gids*, vol. 16, 1969, pp. 214 ff.

[5] E. Tellegen, "Waardevrijheid:toen en nu," *Max Weber. Wetenschap als beroep en roeping*, Alphen a.d. R., 1970, p. 35.

[6] J. Habermas, *Zur Logik der Sozialwissenschaften*, Tübingen, 1967.

[7] O. Duintjer, *art. cit.* in footnote 12 of Chapter 4, p. 30.

[8] O. Duintjer, *loc. cit.*, p. 27.

[9] E. Krieck, *Nationalpolitische Erziehung*, Leipzig, 1935, p. 1.

[10] H. Kelsen, *Reine Rechtslehre*, Vienna, 1934, p. 8. English ed., *Pure Theory of Law*, Berkeley, Calif., 1967.

[11] E. Topitsch, "Sackgassen des Engagements," *Sociologie zwischen Theorie und Empirie*, München, 1970, pp. 135 ff.

CHAPTER 14

[1] R. Shaull, "Maakt onze samenleving revolutie onmogelijk?", *Katernen 2000*, no. 11, vol. 2, Amersfoort, pp. 13 ff.; C. Oglesby and R. Shaull, *Containment and Change*, New York, 1967, quoted after the Dutch ed., 1967, pp. 265 ff.

[2] A. Rich, "Theologie en revolutie," *Wending* vol. 23, 1968, p. 254.

[3] J. Moltmann, *Theologie der Hoffnung*, München, 1967, quoted after the Dutch ed., n.d., pp. 307 ff.

[4] M. Theunissen, *Gesellschaft und Geschichte. Zur Kritik der kritischen Theorie*, Berlin, 1969, pp. 13 ff.

PART TWO

Socio-Critical Essays

1. RELIGION AND CRITIQUE OF SOCIETY

1. The End or the Beginning of Christian Social Thought?

The relationship between religion and politics in our days seems to be rather strange. On the one hand, it is questioned whether Christian social ethics can aspire to a distinct position. What is traditionally called "the social doctrine of the Church" fails to arouse any enthusiasm today, for such a social doctrine is viewed as an ecclesiastical attempt to exercise guardianship. Politics based on religious convictions is simply viewed as a form of clericalism. On the other hand, the Churches are accused of not busying themselves enough with what is happening in society.

At first, the situation is indeed somewhat contradictory. Those who have pronounced the funeral oration over the social doctrine of the Church say that the Christian should remain silent about the affairs of the world because nothing specific can be said about them from the standpoint of faith. On the other hand, precisely as a believer, the Christian thinks that he ought to speak about the affairs of the world because religion without any worldly concerns remains an empty ritual without any real content.

Especially many members of the younger generation criticize the Christian Churches for their political abstention. The call to assume a critical position with respect to society makes itself felt even in theology, where the politically-colored term "the New Left" is also used. Theologians of the New Left relegate many of their colleagues whom orthodox theologians view as left and progressive to the right, the side of petrifaction. Christian social doctrine had barely been buried when its survivors began again to speak of "political theology." Critical theologians even try to develop a "theology of revolution" and a "theology of radicalism."

The situation seems at first to be extremely confused. Orthodox theologians deplore the fact that the value of Christian social doctrine is put into doubt by the progressives. But these progressives, in their turn, are criticized by other progressives because their political liberality actually fosters political aloofness. Many Christian leaders no longer know where they are. Until recently they were accused of meddling if they busied themselves with politics, but now they are accused again—this time of not taking a clear-cut political stance. Nevertheless, there is no contradiction involved in these complaints. We will try to show this by indicating that in these cases matters are viewed in a different perspective, a different field of presence, so that the relationship of religion and politics turns out to be different. Within the framework of the critique of society the interpretation of the relationship between religion and politics is not the same as it is within the context of the traditional social doctrine.

The era of the Christian social doctrine is past and there is no need to bewail its demise. The phenomenon of secularization, which accompanied "the end of conventional Christianity," was not without influence on the conventional Christian view of society. There are few people left today who think that one can draw from Christian religion more or less concrete conclusions about the way society should be constructed. But this is an entirely different matter than claiming that the Christian view of life cannot be of any value for society. One can rightly oppose the position which handles Christian truths as premises in order to deduce from them statements which really pertain to the empirical realm as if they were conclusions. The old Christian social doctrine illegally imported ethical value

judgments into the empirical realm of science. Thus it became an ambiguous mixture of dogmatic *a priori* religious certainties and putative empirical truths.

Contemporary ethical and theological thought realizes that views which in the past were presented as Christian social doctrine based on faith, as a matter of fact had a strongly ideological content. Belief in a kind of specifically Christian theory of society which can be deduced from faith and is the golden mean between liberalism and socialism is dying out, even in Germany, where this doctrine was so thoroughly worked out. Many social theses which were held to be theological data or connected with absolute values and immutable natural laws were in reality nothing but *post factum* safeguards and protective measures favoring existing social structures and power relationships. The fact that many Christians of Europe belonged to the middle class unwittingly gave ideological support to an allegedly Christian social solution in the direction of a more or less colorless in-between, a center-view.[1]

The time is past when Christian faith thought that it possessed a special social doctrine. This is particularly evident from the social encyclicals of the Catholic Church, which held fast to a Christian social doctrine long after the Protestant Churches had abandoned this idea. A comparison of *Rerum Novarum* and *Populorum Progressio* reveals a clear development from a strongly doctrinal attitude to a more pastoral approach. The pastoral constitution on the Church in the modern world of Vatican Council Two also breathes a new spirit. It openly speaks about the autonomous character of the temporal and earthly realm, and it uses the expression "the social doctrine of the Church," so beloved by the older social encyclicals, only once. Of particular importance is that this constitution explicitly recognizes that from their Christian inspiration the faithful can arrive at different ideas and positions with respect to society. No one, it says, may claim a monopoly for his ideas with an appeal to the Gospel or hold that his view alone represents that of the Church. On the contrary, through honest dialogue and exchange of views, people must try to throw light on each other's position. Thus this pastoral constitution confirms a matter which had already be-

come commonly accepted, viz., the idea that there is no specifically Catholic social doctrine derived from faith.

This political neutralization of religion during the past few decades actually is a belated liberalizing emancipation within the Churches. The freedom of politics from religious values can be compared to the freedom of science from values which the Enlightenment had claimed more than two centuries ago. Even as science then freed itself from the theocratic world-view, so now politics tries to become definitively emancipated from ecclesiastical control.

But while the Churches' social doctrine is being buried, Christian radicalism is being born. Especially the younger theology, developed at the University of Münster under the influence of J. Metz, which he—but not all his followers—call "political theology," emphasizes the political consequences of the Christian faith.[2] In this theology the Gospel's function to be critical of society occupies the central position. Its critique of modern "liberal" Christianity is the same as that of the liberal, value-free, science of our time, that is to say, neither science nor religion can assume a socially neutral attitude. A science which thinks that it opts for a value-free standpoint, *de facto* adopts the existing order. That's why the radical theology rightly notes that the political neutrality of the Christian Churches nonetheless has a socio-political meaning in practice. A liberal Church which is politically neutral *de facto* conforms to the existing social system. The net result then is that the well-intented progressive liberalization turns exactly into its opposite. Progress becomes conservative adaptation.

Political theology doesn't wish to be modern but radical. It does not want to adapt the faith to the "modern" world and to update it in this fashion. Its aim is a radical renewal of the existing situation. In the eyes of radical theologians, the liberal tendencies which have appeared in the Catholic Church since Vatican Council Two are anachronistic renewals that occurred elsewhere centuries ago already. Such a liberalization in Catholic circles would have been appropriate to the time of the Enlightenment with its bourgeois idealism and individualism. The Catholic Church is compelled to give up its theological claims on the socio-political realm

and follows the road of the Protestant Churches, which did the same in an earlier stage.

This liberalization, however, doesn't produce a renewal of the Christian Churches themselves. The only thing Christian religion does is to make a convulsive effort to maintain itself within the process of secularization. Religion draws to speculative philosophical positions, ethical dispositions and a pious interior life.[3] It endeavors to perfect the individual. Religion is a private affair and as such divorced from public political life. Although the Churches have given up their socio-political expansionism and view the solution of social problems as a task of secular expertise, their total claims on the personal conscience are emphasized more than ever.

Through this religious "retreat" the Churches unwittingly foster individualism and thus tend to conform to the existing social climate. To work for one's individual religious salvation is wholly in keeping with the liberal mentality of a world in which each one tries to promote his own social and economic position. A religion which is wholly orientated to man's purely inner life implicitly reaffirms the principle and morality of individual achievement prevalent in our society.[4]

The modern world, on its side, is happy to assume a tolerant attitude toward the Christian Churches.[5] Because of their liberal position, they need not be feared any longer politically by the world; at the same time, the Churches' "depolitization" confirms the world's own structure. The "depolitization" and the emphasis on personal religious needs function as substitute mechanisms for the existing social alienation. The sentiments of justice, honesty and solidarity, which are trampled upon on Mondays when work begins, are repressively sublimated on Sundays by religion. The verbal profession of love of fellowmen and of reconciliation in the religious realm offer compensation for the real avarice and antagonistic competition in the profane realm. In this way the inner satisfaction of religious needs becomes a substitute for authentically human and religious needs. Religion is degraded into a consumer-item, something to be enjoyed in one's spare time in exchange for the lack of freedom suffered in the process of labor.

In this fashion the Church functions as a psychoanalytic institute which cures the unsatisfied feelings acquired by man in society. Some American Churches don't hesitate to advertize that they serve the needs of their members better than is done by the competition. The Church is thus too much geared to the individual alone, it doesn't involve society as the cause of the individual's psychical weakness in the process of the cure. Such a practice of Christian love threatens to foster rather than cure the existing alienation because it abstains from submitting society itself to critique. It limits itself to adapting the "unadapted" to the system but fails to subject the system itself to a critical examination.

The younger theologians deserve praise for pointing out the one-sidedness of the modern theology based on existential philosophy, even though it is true that their criticism is still insufficiently accompanied by an empirical analysis. A religion which wishes to maintain itself independently of the social process evaporates into an abstract idealism without concrete objective content. Its exodus from the world is accompanied by an entrance into the community of faith withdrawn from the world and estranged from it. Thus it fosters its own process of decomposition. Radical Christians experience the existing alienation between faith on Sundays and work on Mondays as hypocritical. They rightly criticize a Christianity which is solely concerned with spiritual salvation and neglects earthly involvement.

Radical theology differs from modern existentialistic theology especially in this that it is concerned not only with the conversion of the individual but also with that of society. It aims at a change of mentality but also at a structural change. It wishes to influence the structures indirectly by a change in mentality and an ethico-religious attitude. Radical theology thinks that the faith can also be described directly as social and political activity and not merely indirectly by way of the individual religious disposition. Changes in mentality and structural change have an immediate value for theology. The faith is embodied not only in the religious experience of the individual but also in the reshaping of society.[6]

Through the influence of Marxist thought, the objective social content of the faith is put here more clearly in the foreground.

The political task of the community of Christian believers is based on the theology of history, which holds that God's salvation comes to completion in and through the humanization of the world and society. The Christian hope demands that God's promises be made true in the historical conditions of the present. The radical believer wants to change human history itself into a history of salvation and he can never be satisfied with any given political structure at all. The eschatological expectation evokes the utopian disposition to bring about an ever better society. In this theological perspective the political task becomes a secular "worship" and a profane "consecration."

2. *The Danger of a Revolutionary Orthodoxy*

Contradictions sometimes appear in the new direction taken by Christians with respect to their social responsibility. There are people who attach more value to the words of an authoritative economist or sociologist than to a papal social encyclical; at the same time, however, they would like the Pope to preach the social revolution. On the one hand, so it is said, the Churches often leaned too heavily on their authority in social affairs; on the other, a priest or minister now often uses his position or pulpit to present his own political view to the congregation as a matter of faith.

Some people proclaim that the Gospel in our time demands a Christian-radical politics to the left. Attempts are made, as we saw, to develop a "political theology" and a "theology of the revolution." Such biblical and theological predicates again convey the idea of a monopoly on orthodoxy and thus remain ambiguous. The attempt to preach a revolution as a kind of Church dogma or to sanction a leftist policy with biblical imperatives is like "pouring new wine into old skins." One who tries to justify a political standpoint with biblical or theological arguments lapses into a new kind of clericalism. A political theology easily leads to a new kind of ideological orthodoxy—this time not the conservative but the revolutionary type.

Such "theologizing" of socio-political problems can arise from

different causes. The established Churches can easily become en-
thusiastic about a new-style political theology in the hope of re-
gaining their lost influence. Their political-theological confession of
faith then runs the risk of remaining abstract and purely verbal
while, at the same time, they can beforehand credit Christianity
with any effective improvement resulting from political activity. A
truly left-Christian minority group, on the other hand, is often
induced by its lack of security to put its radical standpoint in a
theological context. When such a minority speaks about a theology
of revolution, it succumbs to the ideological temptation to clothe
its standpoint in the garments of religious absolutes. What it pursues as a minority is thereby theologically proclaimed to be the only
valid position for all. Such a left evangelical charism runs the risk
of becoming uncritical of its own revolutionary activity. For it tries
to raise its own standpoint above all critique when it attempts to
legitimize it through a supracritical dimension, that is to say here,
through God himself. A left-radical position must not be defended
with theological but with socio-political arguments. A critical revolution must resist the temptation to make itself ethically and reli-
giously absolute. A critical attitude demands that one distantiate
oneself also from one's own revolutionary activity and learn if necessary how to relativize it. For otherwise one ends up with a new
kind of establishment and a new conformism, viz., the revolutionary
kind. Man would thus again be self-estranged in the totalitarian
character of the revolutionary impetus.[7]

The attempt to support politics or the revolution by biblical arguments or to legitimize them theologically still takes its starting
point in the old theological framework. The source of all the confusion lies in the fact that renewal continues to be viewed within
the traditional context of thought and thus relapses into the same
old mistake. The question that should be raised is whether the traditional framework itself shouldn't be renewed.

The old framework of thought starts from a Christian "beyond
this world" and tries to spiritualize the profane world from above.
But this theocratic view is only a reflection of the autocratic relationships existing in the society of the past. Christianity, it should

be recalled, has always been strongly interwoven with the existing pattern of society in the past and it occupied there a position of power. This is one of the reasons why the Church thought that it should pronounce a doctrinal judgment about the whole of reality from the standpoint of theology. Because the Church identified itself with the structures of that world, it began to view God as the Creator of a given natural order and itself as acting in His name. This theocratic order was defended by constructing a natural law and a corresponding ethical pattern of norms to which man ought to submit. The traditional social doctrine of the Churches developed from this theocratic standpoint and was defended with an appeal to the natural law given by God himself.

A theology of the revolution or a political theology actually does the same thing all over again, but in a different way. It acts with "enlightenment," by assuming a politically progressive attitude and even wants to avail itself of the approach used by the social sciences. Nevertheless, it relapses into the old theocratic framework of thought by placing its political and scientific position in a biblical and theological context. But a political theology again is an attempt to judge the whole of reality by means of theology; it actually tries to justify secularization from a standpoint beyond secularization. Differently expressed, it assumes a critical standpoint on the basis of an uncritical biblical or ecclesiastical theology. As Trutz Rendtorff rightly remarks, "Even the theology of revolution remains within the framework of renewing the total vision of theology. But such a theology goes counter to every modern attempt to humanize Christian theology and lay out its boundaries. Viewed in this internal-theological context, the theology of the revolution is the latest manifestation of those attempts to give theology again an all-encompassing importance."[8] When matters are considered in this way, one can speak of a revolutionary orthodoxy.

A political theology is from its very inception marked by the same ambiguity as the existentialistic theology of the past few decades. The existentialistic reaction of Christian theology was itself ambivalent. On the one hand, it accepted the autonomous values of the human person, on the other it tried to justify these immanent human values by way of a theological vision of the totality based on transcendent divine values. This same strange ambivalence also appears in political theology.[9] It is a mixture of progressive political autonomy and remnants of an uncritical theology which thinks that it can start from a criterion outside and above the person.[10] The cause of this ambiguity lies in the fact that the Church wants to justify secularization with its theology, while this secularization has not yet been accomplished within the Church itself. As is rightly pointed out in a recent study, "In the present situation it is impossible to give a Christian foundation to a revolutionary critique of society, without first performing a revolutionary critique of the ecclesiastical institution itself."[11]

Before delving deeper into the relationship between the faith and politics in connection with secularization, let us return briefly to the idea of "political theology" developed by J. Metz at the University of Münster. There exists a good deal of terminological confusion in this matter, but we will follow here H. Barion's terminology.[12] Barion distinguishes between "political theology" and "theological politics." He conceives political theology as a theocratic kind of religiousness which thinks that faith should exercise direct power over political reality. The traditional social doctrine of the Churches is a form of political theology in this sense. Barion speaks of "theological politics" when there is a certain political breakthrough and autonomy while there still remains a dogmatic remnant, that is to say, one tries to justify politics with theological arguments. What Barion calls "theological politics" is precisely what Metz calls "political theology." In the preceding consideration of the left-radical standpoint of Christians we have used the term "political theology" in the sense of Metz. But it would be preferable to speak of "theological politics." This theological politics, however, still starts from an unfinished process of secularization.

3. *Christianity from the Standpoint of Secularization*

It is generally recognized today that a radical shift of perspective is taking place even in the realm of religion. A new way of experiencing reality is involved. The image of man and the world-view have become laicized and profane, partly as a result of science and technology. Man has become conscious of his autonomy and freedom with respect to the world. World-view and the image of man are in this respect correlates. Nature has been "humanized" by man and man has been "naturalized" by nature. Contemporary man is more orientated to "this world" than to "beyond this world." It is this Copernican revolution of man's experience of reality that is expressed by the term "secularization." The religious dimension is now often viewed as an impediment to our relationship to the world. In the eyes of many, religion is even an alibi invoked by people who have given up on the world.

For a long time, indeed, Christianity tried to keep away from the influence of the modern world; it withdrew, as it were, into the countryside.[13] But the Christian Churches began to experience problems of "living space" because more and more of its areas were annexed by the secularization of the city. In the past Christianity vainly tried to oppose the "demon" of secularization. This meant that secularization *de facto* became a process of emancipation—a process that was painful from the standpoint of its victims, who called it an unjust annexation, but which the emancipators defended by appealing to the rights of the State, politics, science, progress and the person.

In the past two decades, however, the Christian Churches have reorientated themselves; they no longer view secularization as something anti-Christian, not even as something neutral, but endeavor to explain it as a typical Christian phenomenon. Following F. Gogarten,[14] many writers, such as Harvey Cox[15] and Johann Metz,[16] now claim that secularization did not occur in spite of Christianity but because of it.

The entire process of secularization, they hold, owes its origin to Christianity. The Christian faith with its biblical monotheism precisely stripped the world of its divine character. Its lofty conception of God liberated the earth from earthly gods and thus started the process of secularization. It sounds certainly startling that secularization, which at first was so little appreciated from the standpoint of Christianity, now all of a sudden is claimed to have its very source in the same Christianity. What is the justification for this complete reversal of position?

On historical or *de facto* grounds, it is not easy to give such a justification. For example, in the past few centuries, the Catholic Church certainly did not occupy a vanguard position with respect to the new developments. On the contrary, for a very long time, it did not know what to do with the growing democratic rights of man. In Reformed quarters, influenced in part by Luther's doctrine of the two kingdoms, secularization perhaps had an earlier chance because economic, social and political life was more left to itself. But here, too, the official Church at least often used Luther's doctrine apologetically against secularization.

On the basis of these historical facts a number of writers are willing to concede that the process of secularization has partly been started by values outside Christianity, but they maintain that at least *de jure* secularization belongs to Christianity. In their eyes, secularization is fundamentally and essentially a part of the Christian faith. Such an argument, however, again seems to arise from an opportunistic *a priori* attempt to make Christianity the master-key for every new phenomenon.

Against the various Christian writers who ascribe secularization to Judeo-Christian monotheism, one can with equal or even greater right defend the opposite thesis. Has not the world been stripped of its divine character and has not man come of age, not so much in the name of a biblical transcendent God but rather in the name of man himself, and isn't this precisely the reason why a more refined concept of God could arise?[17] Isn't it true that even the humanism of the Greeks drove the gods ever higher up Mount Olympus?

The entire question of such Christian claims would not be very important if it were not for the fact that we are dealing here with an attempt to put limits to secularization and insert it into the framework of a traditional image of God and the world. Yet the very process of secularization aims precisely at overcoming this image. By making Christianity the explanatory ground of human autonomy, one again endeavors to evaluate human history in terms of a suprahistorical pre-given position, from an objectivistic *a priori* standpoint.

Contemporary man objects precisely to such a supraworld as a "world behind the world," which one can comprehend with a "surveying look." It is uncritical to evaluate the phenomenon of secularization from the standpoint of a Christianity and a Church structure which themselves have not gone through a process of secularization. Many Christian writers who speak of a theological politics, although they recognize the danger of such a "world behind the world," are unable to distantiate themselves consistently from such a world. They do not realize that in this way the religious dimension is too much "humanized" and the human dimension is too much "dehumanized."

For centuries the Christian faith has maintained itself as a closed subculture within the progress of human history. It continued to interpret reality in terms of the medieval cosmological-metaphysical worldview. When in the sixteenth century the anthropological era broke through, a vicious circle arose: on the one hand, the Churches with their antiquated theocratic-cosmic interpretation of the world drove the modern developments on toward atheism; on the other, the anti-religious attitude of modern progress fostered the ghetto mentality of the Churches. Militant atheism reduced all religiousness to subjective projections and viewed religion as an illusion. Feuerbach, Marx, Freud and Jung explained religion through fear, the need for consolation, a slave mentality born from economic need, infantilism and a lack of realism. This aggressive atheism forced the Christianity of that time into a defensive position and made it difficult for it to maintain itself. By its defensive attitude toward atheism, Christianity unwittingly developed a concept of God marked with all the atheistic characteristics of its opponents. For its defense used either one or the other of the following approaches. Either it argued from the known object, trying to prove that many aspects of reality remain unknown to man. Thus God became a stop-gap for man's imperfect knowledge, an unknown factor X in the human system. Or it tried to argue from the side of the subject, pointing to his Promethean pride and temerity, which need to be kept in check by human weakness, such as suffering, illness, death and guilt. In this way God was pictured as a powerful ruler who tries to keep his rebellious servants in their place.

Now that Christianity tries to assume a positive attitude with respect to secularization, it still retains many metaphysical remnants of its old theocratic interpretation of the world. It professes a secularization in terms of Christianity rather than a Christianity in terms of secularization. Christian faith tries to restrict human freedom and political autonomy within a Christian context, while the aim should be precisely a Christianity within the context of man's coming to be man. The Christian Churches still try too much to maintain the faith apologetically *in opposition to* autonomous freedom.

This apologetic standpoint is antiquated today, even though it may perhaps have been appropriate with respect to the secularizing tendencies of the eighteenth and nineteenth centuries. For the perspective of secularization itself has changed. The time of its proud temerity has past. The man of the Enlightenment thought that he could make the whole of reality subject to his understanding and control by his own reason, understood in the sense of scientific reason. In this era there arose a Promethean world-view and man's project of life was too much narrowed down to a project of the world. Now that secularization is becoming more complete, man experiences how powerless he is to give meaning to his own power. Man come of age experiences that secularization is not merely a question of achieving scientific and technological control of the world. Secularization means that we make our being-man true in all its fullness. Perhaps it would be better to speak of fully coming to be man rather than of secularization since the last-named term has too many connotations reminding us of the one-sided technological orientation to the world which was born in the era of the Enlightenment.

Man's project of life doesn't merely consist in being a demi-urgue or *homo faber.* Today's accent lies rather on the ethical relationship, i.e., on being-man for others and on making the world a better dwelling-place on a higher level of being a fellowman. The man who has come of age experiences it as an aspect of his greatness that he himself can take charge of human evolution. But, at the same time, he also becomes conscious of the burden of responsibility involved in this. Society experiences its powerlessness with respect to the developments it has started. Yet, one cannot simply accuse modern man of temerity in this.

Theology must endeavor to give an answer to the questions and problems raised by the continuing secularization. But it cannot do this from without, from a transcendent divine standpoint. Man who has come of age has trouble accepting such a Christianity which claims to possess an immutable and suprahistorical truth and wants to judge social developments in the light of this truth. He doesn't object to such a faith because it is too supernatural but because it is all too natural. He realizes that an antiquated authoritarian structure of society constituted the infrastructure of this ideological-theological superstructure. Only a theology and a Church in which secularization and democratization have been fully accomplished can deal with the meaning and destiny of man's autonomous coming to be himself.[18] But this condition does not yet exist because, on the one hand, the Church still stands outside the process of secularization, and on the other, society itself is still struggling with its democratic coming to be man and, therefore, is still too much estranged from itself.

4. Concluding Remarks

What Christianity will be like in the future or even whether there still will be room for it in a society come of age is difficult to say at present. The radical theologians have pointed out that the future of the Church does not at all lie in a liberal adaptation to the modern world. The Christian faith will become meaningful again only if a Christianity from above gives way to a Christianity coming from the center of the world. The new Christians will not be where the Church is, but the Church will be where these Christians work at building a better society of men.

The radical difference in perspective, then, demands that one do not meet reality with theological or metaphysical absolute truths. The cosmological image of a divine firmament above us, in which Christians until the present century felt spiritually at home, is out of style today. We can no longer find a possible revelation of God above us but only in man's self-development in every realm. The era of a dogmatic theology which from without addressed a message to the world is gone. Only a "deictic" theology, one which tries to speak about God in terms of a man and a society which are becoming themselves, still makes sense.[19] But one shouldn't too quickly think that such a "deictic" theology, as a Christian indication or interpretation of man's destiny, is possible. ("Deictic" comes from the Greek *deiknumi*, to point out, to indicate.)

The radical theologians have rightly emphasized political relevance because it is precisely the political structures which impede the further development of secularization, of man's coming to be man. Several of these theologians rightly also hesitate to imprint a theological label on this tendency because a theology of politics or of revolution unwittingly again leads to a new theological ideology. Such a kind of theologizing easily gives rise to amateurism in politics. A theology of revolution quickly degenerates into what is already sarcastically referred to as "guerilla poetry." The fate of the theology of work, produced only a few years ago, may serve as a warning here. Much of it was rather naive and simply evaporated into vague romanticism.

A religion—including Christianity—need not be reducible to rational concepts, but it ought to remain meaningful. Only that which acts in man's history to renew his existence and his society can lay claim to being meaningful. The urge to theologize about the personal and social praxis of life arises perhaps from uncertainty. One doesn't dare to approach and experience the question whether Christianity still makes sense in our secularizing world as an open question. On the other hand, however, the Christian would also again make the mistake of trying to adapt himself liberally to the modern world if he no longer wishes or dares to ask what Christianity means. The question about the ultimate meaning of secularization itself also remains very problematic in the present phase of human history. And it is also still an open question whether a radical social praxis without a religious faith would not degenerate into a socio-economic ideology or a dogmatic theory of salvation.

2. THE POLITICIAN SHOULD BE NEITHER ANGEL NOR WOLF

1. *Ethical Lyrics in Politics*

In our days the political fronts are becoming active again. There is a widespread conviction that our society demands profound changes. Some people even think and speak about revolution. What is involved here is political conflicts about the existing political system rather than political conflicts within that system. When the political strife is at fever pitch, the shouts arising from the battle field often sound like a strangely ethical lyrics. Sharply split opponents seem to divide society into two kinds of people—the ethically good and the ethically evil. A kind of holy war mentality arises, in which the opposite camp contains only the legion of the damned while one's own camp consists only of the elect.

Those who protagonize radical changes—the Left—accuse their opponents of unconscionable abuse of power. But before making such a grave moral accusation, one surely should be beyond all reproach oneself. The Right, in their turn, accuse the radicals of unconscionable extremism; they forget that such a moral anathema may be cast only by one who himself is without spot or wrinkle.

Political battle becomes naive when political factions attack one another with moral epithets which, at most, can find application in the individual sphere. Yet it is a fact that political standpoints are often adorned with ethical slogans that would make even angels cry. One faction calls the other untrustworthy crooks and, while sticking this label on the backs of its opponents, tries to sell its own lily-white uprightness to the voters. One group claims that it has taken up the political challenge out of sheer concern for the public interest and the common good, thereby conveying that its opponents are moved by self-interest and are immorally trying to make politics serve their selfish designs. One party claims to assume an "impartial" position—but how can any party manage to be impartial? The opposite party feels morally offended by that claim because it is accused of not being "impartial"—but why should a party blush for being called partial?

At first, it may seem to be only a source of amusement that in the political combat one party adorns itself with ethical merit badges while stripping its opponents of theirs. But there is also an aspect in this that gives rise to concern. Ethical puritanism, as history shows, easily leads to a crusader's mentality which makes one parade as a hero or a martyr because one does violence to fellowmen considered to be heretics. Political leaders who claim to act in the name of God or on the basis of a high ethical ideal usually turn out to be tyrants who can maintain themselves only by making victims.

Now that political competition runs high and everyone in his turn releases his tensions and aggressions in ethical lyrics, it is useful to take a closer look at the ethical phrases used by political antagonists. Political philosophy can do its share to prevent the struggle from becoming embittered and keep it clean without removing its aggressive character. What is ultimately involved is the relationship between ethics and politics. The question to be asked is whether it makes sense to use moral norms which primarily apply to the personal level for political activities which are primarily a group happening. Doesn't such a use lead to hypocrisy and impede effective policies?

2.   *The Relativity of the Political View*

In the political arena it is often forgotten that man as a knowing subject doesn't have a standpointless standpoint. This idea can perhaps be useful to clarify the rules of political competition. We do not wish to suggest that political opponents should restrict themselves to patting each other on the back, but only that they should abstain from invoking the Lord and crusading in his name.

Political philosophy wishes to point out that, in pursuing political values and goals, one should retain a certain playfulness and not take oneself too seriously because otherwise one can easily get lost in ideological exaggerations. A politician should be able playfully to distantiate himself from his own political view. Such playfulness does not at all mean that one assumes an attitude of resignation or lacks social commitment. On the contrary, it is the distinguishing characteristic of a critical attitude and a mature freedom. One who allows a certain amount of elbowroom between himself and his standpoint remains conscious of the relativity of his own vision, no matter how deeply he gets involved.

The politician who cannot playfully distantiate himself replaces earnest combat by fanatical struggle. He makes an ideological fetish of his political view. Such fanatics are found not only among arch-conservatives but equally among arch-progressives. That's why today's fanatic rebel can easily become tomorrow's oppressive tyrant. History shows this all too eloquently with respect to most violent revolutions. Only the politician who does not become dogmatically fixed but retains a certain irony in the political battle understands his profession as an art, that is to say, he knows how to play his part in the power play in order to achieve whatever is attainable. Irony is a play about which Plato long ago observed that it imitates divine creativity on the human scale.

We find ourselves here in the heart of the political phenomenon, which is the relativity of political truth and political views. Man sees every truth, including those on the political level, in a *particular* perspective. He can see and approach the general well-being of the entire people only from his own social and socio-economic situation. The politically "right" answer is always colored by this life situation. The rationalism of the eighteenth and nineteenth centuries thought that man could determine his political choice in a perfectly rational way. But such a *homo politicus* has never existed, just as there never was a *homo economicus*. Because the economic, social and cultural situation of all members of a political system is not the same, it follows that not everyone will view the future of society in a uniform fashion. And because knowledge is codetermined by personal and group interest, it is not possible to indicate exactly what is the best for the whole of a society.

To the extent that people don't dare to admit that their stand-point is codetermined by their own interest, they often resort to proclaim their position as the Good with a capital G. With an appeal to ethical objectivity and disinterestedness they push their own selfish interests into the background. A politician, however, who demands an ethical monopoly for his standpoint acts as if there were suprahistorical ethical norms.[1] Precisely in this he offends against ethics. Genuine ethical rationality starts from the supposition that there exists a dialectical tension between norm and fact, between utopia and facticity. A critical ethics will avoid two extremes. First of all, it will never defend any human reality as the perfect good; it will not preverve the *status quo* at the expense of change. If it did that, it would identify the norm with the fact and emasculate the utopian impetus. Secondly, ethical rationality refuses to give *a priori* approval to any revolutionary change simply because it is a radical change; for otherwise it would universally justify every revolution. The critical will to change has to take into account the possibility that the change can also be brought about, articulated and moti-vated in a different fashion. A revolutionary change is neither more nor less than a special kind of change, and as such it must be examined also with respect to the social structures which it implies.[2] When this is not done, one falls into the opposite extreme and attempts to deduce the situation from norms existing in themselves. The utopian vision then degenerates into an authoritarian ideology. Any policy which directly appeals to so-called ethical values to present its standpoint as the only morally right position does not proceed in a critical fashion but acts despotically and lapses into an orthodoxy of either the right or the left.

The political option lies at the intersection of ethical convictions or values and a situation which allows a limited range of possibilities. Although science can make a contribution to a more rational understanding of the values, alone it can never lead to a solution of the problem of choice.[3] This means that the political choice amounts to no more than an opinion. That's why it is wrong to remove confrontation and dialogue between different opinions from the realm of politics, even though many tensions result from this confrontation. As long as groups of different political persuasions are willing to strive for a real improvement of society, it would be wrong to refuse a dialogue with them. Political discussion is meaningless only with groups which act in a repressive and intolerant way and show that they have made their decisions already in an authoritarian fashion.[4] That's why in a nation possessing a certain political maturity the improvement of its future well-being is best served by a system of political parties. We do not mean a bureaucratic system of parties, in which the voters only now and then are passively allowed to vote, but parties which really speak for their members and see to it that the members share in a constant and free discussion.

The perspectivistic character of human knowledge means that in political matters man's understanding assumes a specific form of its own. What we mean is that the confrontation of conflicting standpoints between political factions also has the character of a power rivalry. One would have to be politically very naive to think that communication between different political options through mere dialogue leads to relevant results. Politics is and remains an interest and power struggle. To be successful in politics, people must constitute a group and make use of power. One who wishes to convince the other parties of his right by moral arguments alone does not go very far. Few political conversions ever result from such an approach. Politics is mainly a struggle between different social groups and especially in the context of the group it is evident that "man is also a desire." Every political group tries to attain more power and prosperity for itself at the expense of others. The emancipation of an oppressed group succeeds only if the oppressed as an organized power can press their demands.

On the political level one should not preach a morality of love, which primarily applies to interpersonal relationships. It would be hypocritical to do so and hardly be successful.[5] The morality of the political group has its own "rules of the game." Even Martin Luther King thought that little social justice is brought about by merely appealing to ethical sentiments and rational persuasion. It may sound harsh to a political idealist, but politics is also a justified interest and power struggle. Especially as a member of a group, man is not all sweet reasonableness. Precisely the realization that every group also wants power and serves its own interest makes it possible for all to recognize this fact and to humanize the power confrontation by political rules of the game. And the one who is most eager to get power is the moral puritan who thinks that he acts politically without any selfishness.

On the one hand, the political party is an interest group. Its task is to represent the interests of its constituency and defend them against the interests of other groups. On the other hand, the political group must fit its interest into that of society as a whole and let itself be governed by the over-all interest as a norm. But here, too, there is a dialectical relationship. The interest must be justified by what is right, yet the underlying view of what is right is also colored by the self-interests which occupy the foreground of one's attention. It would be hypocritical to seek a puritanical escape from acknowledging group interest through lofty idealizations. But it is also dishonest cynically to distort ideal norms to make them serve group interests.

3.   *The True Political Ethos*

The ambivalence of man, who is neither an angel nor a wolf, shows itself especially in the political realm. If groups pursue only their own interest without taking those of others into account, politics becomes a brutal struggle for power. One man or one group would then be nothing but a wolf for the other, and political morality would degenerate into cynicism. But as a rational being man is also concerned with morality and wants to let the good of the whole society codetermine his own political interest. Every party as a party of interests ought to possess a superstructure of ideas. It should have an ethical inspiration, even if this inspiration needs to be translated into political terms.[6]

A party politician who claims that only purely ideal motives make him aim at the common good tries to occupy a standpointless standpoint. He acts as if he were an angel. He forgets that he does not possess the purity of an angel and can look at the social ideal of

man only from a certain perspective, that is to say, from the standpoint of his group. He can view political truth in its totality only
through the colored spectacles of his own particular situation and
interests. A party which one-sidedly appeals to a too lofty ethical
motivation forgets that it is also an interest and power party. It
behaves as if it were the umpire of the political struggle and forgets that it is a party which participates in the political game.

This sort of puritanism must be kept out of politics. Although
undoubtedly the ethical values are an important background factor in political activity, they should not be directly appealed to
but only find expression in an indirect way as translated into the
political contest. The ethical inspiration must be expressed in concrete political statements and also in concrete strivings for power.
Political puritanism is fundamentally a profane form of clericalism. A politician who dresses in such an ethical garment wrongly
thinks that he is endowed with a "surveying glance" by which he
can see the common interest "in itself." Such a political "angel,"
displaying a Platonic paternalism, is rightly regarded with distrust
by his political opponents. He usually conceals a number of dangerous torpedos under his wings.

All this is not a plea for a pedestrian form of politics. Politics
is the art of the possible, not merely the technically possible but
what is possible for man as man. In politics also ideas and views
play an important role. But these ideas should not be borrowed
from a lofty individual ethics. A political view which aims ethically
too high remains an ill-advised view. Political idealism can work
politically only when it is in touch with a particular historical context of a political society.

Politics is not merely a matter of power and interest groups.
Every party must let its particular interests be governed by the value
of the common well-being. It is a party of ideas only in this sense
that it tries to justify its power and aims by means of what is just for
society at large. Conversely, the party must realize that its ideas are
also ideologically colored because it represents a number of private interests.[7] What it views as right for society at large is marked
and distorted by its own private power position.[8]

Ideas must inspire political activities, but they must also be constantly subjected to critical reflection. For otherwise they easily become an incarnation of a political lie. Marx's Communist Manifesto already noted that the ruling ideas of a period are merely the ideas of the ruling class. All too easily an established group can use ideas and values to camouflage purely private interests. On the other hand, there is no reason why an oppressed class which opposes itself to the ruling class should not candidly admit that its own ideas also arise from a desire for power. Unavoidably, what is right is politically realized only with the aid of power.

4. *Competitive Pursuit of Politics*

Truth is always approached from a perspective. Political truth, understood as the right development of society in its totality, also is always viewed from different sides. A politician who thinks that he can avoid this one-sidedness acts as if he were an emissary from heaven. And one who doesn't even realize that there is a possibility of being one-sided acts as a tyrant sent by hell. A sincere political vision of the total societal process does not mean a conscious or unconscious falsification of the truth, but is truth as "viewed," and as such always also remains an estranged truth because morally man's "hands are always dirty." The dialectician teaches the politician that the partial interest is always understood in terms of the common interest, and vice versa.

On the ethical and religious levels this dialectics demands a peaceable communication. Only through a loving dialogue between each other's standpoints is it possible to arrive at a better insight into ethical and religious truths. This should not be understood as if political party chairmen should engage in political ecumenism. That would be as strange as soccer players who, instead of kicking the ball, try to caress it. Politics inevitably is a strange mixture of right and power, but right has to justify power and power has to bring right.[9]

Communication between political standpoints has a competitive rather than dialogical character. Truly democratic politics must remain a healthy aggressive contest. A truly political contest is incompatible with an immature mentality which views issues involving the destiny of nations as nothing more than a political football game. It likewise excludes the immature attitude which inflates one's own ideas into slogans for a holy war crusade. The politics of a democratic society is best served when this politics is subjected to critique in the form of an open and frank competition between the groups existing in that society. Politics also demands that the antagonists be more or less equally matched in their abilities because in this way the best possible political results will be attained.

3. THE CRISIS OF THE UNIVERSITY PROFESSOR

1. *Critical Consciousness*

The temples of science and scholarship, known as universities, today resound with calls for critical science, critical theories and critique of society. Even the entering freshman knows that he must assume a critical attitude toward society. And he will at once join the chorus of critique, even though there are many dissonant, uncritical notes in his attempts to carry the tune.

What is the reason for the complaint that the university, that age-old fortress of knowledge, doesn't have today enough critical firing power? Why is it that precisely such a young science as sociology has failed to foresee today's social tensions? Why are certain young people, despite their frequent lack of experience, often better able to point out the symptoms of disease than are many learned men with impressive records of achievement? Why is there need for such a call for critical pursuit of science if we keep in mind that science itself can exist only by being critical?

Critique is connected with crisis. A crisis indicates a critical situation; a decisive point is reached and the further development from there on can take a positive or negative turn. In this sense we speak of a puberty crisis, the crisis of an illness, a spiritual crisis, a political crisis, etc. In each case the term refers to a situation which implies a critical turning point and demands a critical decision. For example, the spiritual crisis is a certain phase in a person's life. He lives on the boundary between two worlds. His old world of convictions with their familiar pattern of thought no longer speaks to him, but the new life-world is not yet fully born. A man in a spiritual crisis swings anxiously between two worlds in an attempt to finds his bearings and certainty. He lives in a situation of critical growth. Can the new world fully develop in him, so that he will be spiritually reborn, or will his resilience be broken because the new life cannot break through the heavy crust of petrified patterns and ends up by being asphyxiated? The striking aspect of such cases is that judgment and decision (in Greek *krinein*) are made from within the crisis situation and the crisis process.[1]

In Antiquity critique and crisis went together. The Greeks spoke about "critique" especially in reference to the verdict in a court of justice. In a crisis a judgment was made as in a lawsuit. The Romans spoke about "critique" in the medical sense as the evaluation of the crisis of a disease. In the Gospel of St. John the term "critical" has a theological sense and refers to the crisis of salvation history with its separation between the elect and the damned. But with the rise of the sciences in the eighteenth and nineteenth centuries "critical" lost its connection with "crisis." The Enlightenment thought that it proceeded critically if it evaluated the situation without prejudices and, as much as possible, as a neutral spectator from *without*. The scientific tradition of the Enlightenment, which still strongly influences science today, wants to proceed in an unprejudiced and value-free way.

Viewed in the light of the history of its time, the Enlightenment's attempt can be understood and even praised. Enlightened thought rightly threw away the prejudices of the antiquated religious and philosophical world-view, which from without and from above imposed value judgments on the pursuit of science. It objected to the belief in authority which had prevailed in the feudal society. But the prejudice of the Enlightenment is itself a prejudice against all prejudices. Its ideology consists in its belief that all presuppositions can be eliminated.

If one equates being critical with making a judgment independently of the social framework and without occupying any selective standpoint, then one *de facto* occupies a subjectivistic and rational-istic standpoint. One then adheres to the ideology of individual-ism, which is the value schema of bourgeois society. This "bourgeois" form of critique has lost its connection with crisis. While originally a critical standpoint was sought in terms of the crisis, the critical situation and the social framework, now one tries to judge social reality in terms of a subjectivistic and individualistic standpoint. Such an attempt to pursue value-free science unwittingly relies on the bourgeois ideology of individualism.

Today it is increasingly realized that all our thinking and acting are based on socio-cultural presuppositions. Even science is implic-itly based on a view of man and society. It is within this context of ideas that all human projects receive their meaning and direc-tion. The horizon of the world-view is literally most original; it constitutes the origin, the source from which every thing springs and comes about. Human consciousness is a normative conscious-ness. Science also is in its essence and structure dominated and guided by value principles. Scientific thought starts from, and is supported by value presuppositions. These fundamental value-ideas constitute, as it were, the atmosphere in which the sciences breathe. That's why the interpretation of scientific data must always be integrated into the broader framework of a social system of val-ues.

It is easy to fall for the idea that we can think and act in a value-free way because the spiritual atmosphere is not visible. The hori-zon of presuppositions itself is not immediately visible; it becomes visible only in an indirect way insofar as our actions start from this horizon as their background. The fundamental pattern of values and ideas is not itself something given but it is included in all our given interpretations and systems.

As J. Walgrave explains in an inspiring article,[2] our world of thought has two levels. There are, first of all, unconscious or pre-conscious ideas, so-called "source ideas." These ideas are the springs from which flows the movement of our thinking. Secondly, there are "object ideas," that is to say, ideas about which we argue and have discussions. The background of the "source ideas" unwittingly animates the "object ideas" to which we pay explicit attention.

2.   *The Contemporary "Crisis of Foundations"*

The background against which we act easily escapes our attention. The fundamental ideas thus readily become unquestioned and accepted assumptions. We unwittingly breathe the "spirit of the times" just as we unwittingly breathe the air in our environment. Moreover, the idea of allegedly value-free inquiry fostered by enlightened thinking makes us uncritical with respect to the social roots of our thought. That's why our natural "forgetfulness" of the value background assumes the form of repression.

Today, however, we can no longer breathe that ideological air unwittingly because it has become too polluted. Our society is full of contradictions and injustices. The traditional values are unmasked as ideologies and lose their obviousness. We live therefore in a crisis situation. The old collective ideas no longer satisfy, but the new ones are not yet fully visible. We face the critical decision of either continuing along the old lines and getting mired even more deeply or trying to find our way gropingly in a new direction.

The social sciences in particular feel the vehemence of this crisis. The fundamental pattern on which the classical and neoclassical trends in economics and the structural-functionalistic trends in sociology are based no longer meet the bill. The call for critique of society and critical theory are the expression of a desire to pursue the social sciences in the light of new "source ideas," new inspirations. There is a tendency to study social reality in a new perspective and against a different horizon.

The history of scientific thought shows that discoveries do not easily result from horizontal research, which merely relocates the boundaries of knowledge farther away on the same plane. Fundamental discoveries are made when at a given moment reality is approached from a vertically different standpoint. As Th. Kuhn has shown this is so even in the history of the physical sciences. In his book, *The Structure of Scientific Revolutions*, he describes how in physical science also true progress occurred only when at a given moment a new "paradigm," a new way of thinking, became the starting point of research.[3] From time to time every science experiences a crisis about its foundations. A new perspective is then opened up upon the phenomena, and the scientific data are viewed in a different light. Heidegger speaks in this connection about a new ontological field of presence, by which the ontic-scientific inquiry is led to enter entirely new paths. He cites Galileo, Newton, Bohr and Heisenberg as examples, but one could add the names of Darwin, Marx, Freud, Einstein and others to this list.[4]

A new theory does not originate by the accumulation of knowledge according to the old theory. At most, a number of ontic elements in the existing field of presence can become the occasion for formulating a new field of presence. The new way of looking at the phenomena gains in convincing power if it turns out to offer a better approach to them. Kuhn shows that younger men of science are more open to this new approach than the older ones, who are inclined to take a negative attitude. The result then is the well-known struggle between schools of thought, of which history offers numerous examples. Such a conflict usually is full of misunderstandings because the opponents speak in terms of different frameworks.

What Kuhn and Heidegger say on historical grounds about the "crisis of foundations" in science finds its confirmation in our times. Sociology is afflicted by the struggle between the new dialectical approach and the established structural functionalism. The economic renovators belong to the camp of the dialecticians and neo-Marxists, who oppose the accepted neo-classical theories. The new theories, as we have said, want to proceed in a way that is critical of society.

3. *Critical and Uncritical Critique of Society*

Young people and, in particular, young men of science have a knack for discovering new, unused possibilities in our society. In their scientific work they assume a critical standpoint with respect to society. They demand that science be value-conscious and "committed."

The critique of society and the critical theory want to check scientific theory constantly with respect to its implicit social presuppositions. The call for critique expresses the desire not to start from unquestioned ideological assumptions, but to let the fundamental ideas be permanently in a state of crisis through constant reflection. A science which does not critically reflect on the ideas from which it springs proceeds in an uncritical fashion.

This critique of society, however, itself can also be uncritical. The utopian thinker can act just as dogmatically as the traditionalist. For the "source ideas" are not themselves given in a thematic way, they are not "object ideas." These "source ideas" become apparent only when they are critically articulated by scientific reflection. Science without critique of society leads to neurotic repression, but a critique of society which does not receive a scientific shape leads to a manic psychosis. Scientific research which is not animated by utopian values leads to man's estrangement in the *status quo*, but the utopia which does not find a critical-scientific articulation leads to man's self-estrangement in a dogmatic illusion. On the one hand, scientific analysis must be critically understood in the light of an overarching inspiring image of society as synthesis, on the other, this image of society, in its turn, must be critically analyzed by science.

The question that remains to be asked is whether constant critique on society will make it possible to prevent sudden modifications of the life-world in the future. The call for permanent revolution and permanent education makes some people expect that in the future qualitative changes need no longer be abrupt and tempestuous. The big question, however, is whether it will ever be possible for man to let life run its course in all its aspects with perfect "rationality."[5] It would appear unreasonable to start from such great expectations about man's rationality, for they could make us insensitive to qualitative changes. Permanent revolution and permanent education however, can lead us to an earlier discovery of the right moment for making a critical turn, so that the new field of presence can come about more expeditiously and less painfully.

Many people today draw their inspiration from Marx, and rightly so, for in Marx one can already find the fundamental tendency of contemporary critical theory. Marx wanted to exercise critique in the light of the existing crisis. He aimed at a scientific socialism and thus became the first modern critic of society. He wanted both to pursue science critically in the light of a socialistic image of society and critically to analyze this socialistic image as a "source idea" in the light of science. That's why he spoke of scientific socialism.

Marx, moreover, emphasized that the economic dimension of existence strongly influences all domains of human life and thought. Today we realize that the prevailing capitalistic system has evil effects on many levels of life. Capitalism forces people to compete and thus fosters individualism and aggression. It is closely allied to economic imperialism. Its one-sided emphasis on production and achievement exercises influence on education, and the system fosters discrimination against races and women.

Many thinkers feel attracted by Marx's fundamental ideas, even though much of his economic theory is now antiquated. The attraction lies in Marx himself rather than in Marxism. A critical theory must not simply reproduce Marx's basic view, it must productively translate his view into a contemporary form. It should understand Marx better than Marx understood himself.

4. *The Crisis of the University Professor*

The university crisis is fundamentally a crisis of society. The "source ideas" of progressive students no longer are in harmony with those of most professors. A new and younger generation of students and teachers wants to change society in the light of new "source ideas." They oppose many professors whose theories start from thought patterns that appear of doubtful value to them.

The transition from an old to a new value pattern is always a painful existential conflict. One floats between two worlds without any anchorage. Many professors are at their wits' end. The foundation of their social theories sinks away under the unmasking critique of their students. Because they are not yet sensitive to the new values, they often cling desperately to the old framework and try to steady themselves by the authority of their professorial chairs.

Yet a dialogue is necessary if the crisis is to lead to a critical decision. Whether we like it or not, a younger generation is more expert in sensitivity to a new pattern of values. On the other hand, these young people need the expertise of the professorial ranks for the critical articulation of a new society in the light of their socialistic inspiration. The professor needs to step down from his lofty chair and be willing to learn from his students. And the student needs to become conscious of the fact that a university education implies a systematic and scientific approach, about which the professor knows more than he does. The crisis of the university professor bears a certain resemblance to that of the priest in the Catholic Church. Until recently, professor and priest held positions in which they exercised their functions with authority from a pulpit or a chair, dressed in cassock and sometimes in academic gown as badge of their authority. Few priests wear cassocks today and they feel less need to exercise their function from a pulpit. The time will soon come when the professor, too, will descend from his lofty chair and surrender the badge of his authority.

Notes—Part Two

CHAPTER 1

[1] B. de Clercq, *Godsdienst en ideologie in de politiek*, The Hague, 1966, pp. 77 ff.

[2] J. Metz, *Zur Theologie der Welt*, München, 1968.

[3] J. Klapwijk, *Tussen historisme en relativisme*, Assen, 1970, pp. 434 ff.

[4] T. Rendtorff, "De opbouw van een revolutionaire theologie. Een analyse van de structuur," *Theologie der revolutie*, Baarn, 1968, p. 60.

[5] For a critique of liberal theology see the periodical *Tegenspraak*, especially nos. 1, 3 and 6 of the first volume, 1969-70.

[7] A. Rich, *art. cit.* in footnote 2 of Chapter 14, pp. 254 ff.

[8] T. Rendtorff, *loc. cit.*, p. 68.

[9] J. Klapwijk, *op. cit.*, p. 440.

[10] T. Rendtorff, *loc. cit.*, p. 66.

[11] *Tegenspraak*, Jan. 1970, p. 51.

[12] H. Barion, " 'Weltgeschichtliche Machtsform?' Eine Studie zur politischen Theologie des II. Vatikanischen Konzils," *Epirrhosis. Festgabe für Carl Schmitt*, Berlin, 1968, p. 14. See also B. van Onna, "100 jaar onfeilbaarheid," *Tegenspraak*, July, 1970, p. 22.

[13] M. Plattel and M. Rijk, "Het geseculariseerd mens- en wereldbeeld in verband met het godsdienstig verschijnsel," *Sociale wetenschappen*, vol. 10, 1967, pp. 281 ff.

[14] F. Gogarten, *Verhängnis und Hoffnung der Neuzeit*, Stuttgart, n.d., p. 103.

[15] H. Cox, *The Secular City*, New York, 1965, quoted after Dutch ed., Utrecht, 1966, p. 27.

[16] J. Metz, "Weltverständnis im Glauben," *Geist und Leben*, vol. 35, 1962, pp. 165 ff.

[17] A. Peperzak, *Techniek en dialoog*, Delft, 1967, p. 8.

[18] A. Danenberg, "De klemmende vraag van de secularisatie aan de theologie," *Tijdschrift voor theologie*, vol. 8, 1968, pp. 170 ff.

[19] A. Danenberg, *art. cit.*, p. 181.

CHAPTER 2

[1] C. Schmitt, "Die Tyrannei der Weste," *Säkularisation und Utopie. Erbracher Studien*, Stuttgart, 1967, pp. 37 ff.

[2] T. Rendtorff, "Ethiek en revolutie. Een kritische confrontatie," *Theologie der revolutie*, Baarn, 1968, p. 110.

[3] A. Brecht, *Political Theory, the Foundations of Twentieth Century Political Thought*, Princeton, 1959. H. Daudt, *Enige recente ontwikkelingen in de wetenschap der politiek*, Leiden, 1963, p. 17.

[4] T. Rendtorff, *loc. cit.*, p. 110.

[5] H. Achterhuis, "Inclusief denken. Bestseller over een nieuwe term voor een oude zaak," *De nieuwe linie*, vol. 25, August 8, 1970, p. 5.

[6] L. de Rijk, "Een kritische reflectie op het verschijnsel politiek," *Tijdschrift voor Filosofie*, vol. 31, 1969, pp. 60 ff.

[7] B. de Clercq, *op. cit.*, in footnote 1 of Part Two, Chapter 1, pp. 51 ff.

8 R. Beerling, *Kratos. Studies over macht*, Amsterdam, 1956, pp. 167 ff. M. Rijk, "Geweld als onmacht," *Opvoeding*, vol. 18, 1968, pp. 34 8 ff.

9 B. de Clercq, *op. cit.*, pp. 58 ff.

CHAPTER 3

1 R. Koselleck, *Kritik und Krise*, Freiburg, 1959, pp. 189 ff. J. Habermas, *Theorie und Praxis*. Neuwied, 1963, pp. 179 ff.

2 J. Walgrave, "De cultuurcrisis van onze tijd," *Kultuurleven*, vol. 36, 1969, pp. 761 ff.

3 T. Kuhn, *The Structure of Scientific Revolutions*, Chicago, 1962.

4 M. Heidegger, *Holzwege*, Frankfurt a.M., 1957, pp. 50 and 179; *Vorträge und Aufsätze*, Pfullingen, 1954, pp. 45 ff. O. Duintjer, *De vraag naar het transcendentale*, Leiden, 1966, pp. 364 ff.

5 M. Theunissen, *Gesellschaft und Geschichte*, Berlin, 1969, pp. 13 ff.

Index of Names

Index of Subject Matter